BARBECUES
AND SALADS

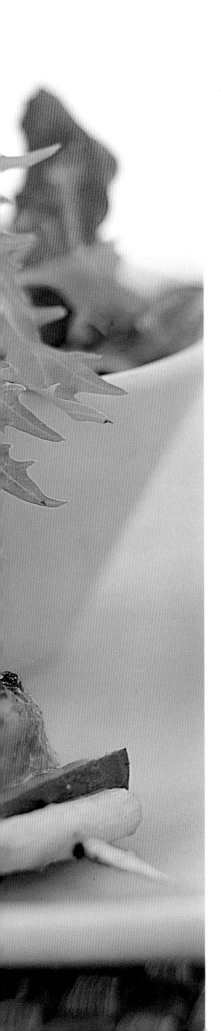

BARBECUES
AND SALADS

CONTENTS

Orange and Ginger Glazed Ham, page 99.

Barbecued Lobster Tail with Avocado Sauce, page 94.

Corn on the Cob with Tomato Relish, page 115.

Pork Sausage Burger with Mustard Cream, page 27.

All recipes in this book have been double-tested.

When we test our recipes, we rate them for ease of preparation. The following cookery ratings are on the recipes in this book, making them easy to use and understand.

A single Cooking with Confidence symbol indicates a recipe that is simple and generally quick to make – perfect for beginners.

Two symbols indicate the need for just a little more care and a little more time.

Three symbols indicate special dishes that need more investment in time, care and patience—but the results are worth it.

NOTES
International conversions and a glossary containing unfamiliar terms can be found on page 208. Cooking times may vary slightly depending on the individual oven. We suggest you check the manufacturer's instructions to ensure proper temperature control.

BARBECUE BASICS

Some barbecues can be as formal as a dinner party, others as relaxed as a picnic on the beach.
Whatever the case, you will need to be prepared—choose the barbecue that suits you best, light
the perfect fire and prepare the food to its maximum advantage.

TYPES OF BARBECUES

Fuel-burning

Fixed barbecue Many gardens contain some sort of fixture for barbecuing; they are relatively simple constructions, usually made from bricks or cement and featuring two grills—the bottom for building the fire, the top for cooking the food. These grills are not generally height-adjustable, so cooking can only be regulated by adjusting the fire, or moving the food away from or towards the fire. Being fixed these barbecues cannot, of course, be moved to shelter from high winds or rain. Despite this, fixed barbecues are easy to use and maintain, and quite often are large enough to cater for big gatherings.

Weber/ Kettle barbecue A popular style of portable barbecue, the weber has a close-fitting lid and air vents at top and bottom which allow for greater versatility and accuracy in cooking. Webers can function either as a traditional barbecue, as an oven or as a smoker (see panel on page 9 for preparation techniques). Weber barbecues only burn charcoal or heat beads (wood is not recommended) and are relatively small. The standard diameter is 57 cm, so if barbecuing for large groups more than one weber is probably required.

Brazier This is the simplest style of fuel-burning barbecue, of which the small, cast iron hibachi is probably best known. A brazier consists of a shallow fire-box for burning fuel with a grill on top. Some grills are height adjustable or can rotate. Braziers are best fitted with a heat-reflecting hood, so that food will cook at an even temperature.

Gas or Electric Barbecues

Although often more expensive, these barbecues are very simple to use. They do not require an open flame, only connection to their heat source. In most cases, the gas or electricity heats a tray of reusable volcanic rock. Hickory chips can be placed over the rock-bed to produce a smoky flavour in the food, if desired. Sizes of models vary, the largest being the wagon style, which usually features a workbench, reflecting hood and, often, a bottom shelf for storage. While small portable gas models, which require only the connection of a gas bottle, are greatly manoeuvrable, electric models are, of course, confined to areas where mains electricity is available. Most gas or electric barbecues have temperature controls; their accuracy is their primary advantage. Electric models can be fitted with rotisseries or spit turners for spit roasting.

THE FIRE
Fuel

Although traditional, wood is not an ideal fuel for cooking. It can be difficult to light and burns with a flame. Charcoal or heat beads are preferable. They will create a bed of glowing heat which is perfect for cooking. They do not smell, smoke

A weber barbecue, although compact, can prepare a variety of foods.

or flare and are readily available in supermarkets or hardware shops. (Heat beads are sometimes known as barbecue briquettes and should not be confused with heating briquettes, which are not suitable for cooking.)

Firelighters are essential for lighting charcoal or heat bead fires. They are soaked in kerosene so will ignite instantly. Do not attempt to cook while firelighters are still burning, as they give off kerosene fumes. Generally one or two

A gas-fuelled wagon barbecue featuring hood and work areas.

firelighters will inflame about twenty pieces of charcoal or heat beads.

A 'normal' fire consists of about 50–60 heat beads or pieces of charcoal and will last for several hours. All recipes in this book can be cooked over a normal fire.

Preparation

Once lit, fires should be left to burn for about 40–50 minutes before cooking. Heat beads or charcoal will become pale and develop a fine, ash coating when they are ready to use. (Wood will have a low flame and have begun to char.) If preparing a weber (kettle) barbecue, leave off the lid while the fire is developing.

Build the fire in the middle of the grate, so that cooked food can be moved to the edge of the grill and kept warm.

Temperature control

A fire's temperature can be lowered by damping down with a spray of water. (A trigger-style plastic spray bottle is ideal.) Damping also produces steam which puts moisture back in the food.

The best and safest way to increase the heat of a fire is to add more fuel and wait for the fire to develop. Do not fan a fire to increase its heat; this will only produce a flame. Never pour flammable liquids on a fire.

Coals ready for cooking: Beads have developed a fine ash coating.

Cooking techniques

Most recipes in this book call for the food to be cooked over a direct flame. Indirect cooking is only possible on weber (kettle) barbecues. (See panel on page 9 for how to prepare a barbecue for indirect cooking.)

Direct Cooking

As with grilling or frying in the kitchen, the less turning or handling of the food the better. Once the fire is ready, lightly brush the grill or flatplate with oil. Place the food over the hottest part of the fire and sear quickly on both sides; this retains moisture. Once seared move food to a cooler part of the grill or flatplate to cook for a few more minutes. Barbecuing is a fast-cooking process so even well-done food will not take long. Techniques such as stir-frying are ideal for the barbecue flatplate.

Test meat for doneness by firmly pressing it with tongs or the flat edge of a knife. Meat that is ready to serve should 'give' slightly but not resist pressure too easily. At first, the degree of doneness may be difficult to judge, but try to resist cutting or stabbing the meat; this not only reduces its succulence, but releases juices which may cause the fire to flare. Pork and chicken should not be served rare, so if in any doubt as to doneness remove to a separate plate and make a slight cut in the thickest part of the meat. If the juices do not run clear, return to the heat for further cooking. Test fish for

Retain moistness in the meat by searing quickly and turning once only.

Test meat for 'doneness' by pressing gently with tongs.

doneness by gently flaking back the flesh in the thickest part with a fork. Cooked flesh should be white and opaque, but still moist.

Smoking

Smoking chips or chunks come from hickory wood, mesquite, dried mallee root, red-gum or acacia trees and are available from barbecue specialists and some hardware or variety stores. Their smoke provides an extra and unusual flavour to the food.

Smoking is best done on a covered barbecue (see panel on page 9) but can also be done on an open fire. Scatter smoking wood throughout the coals. Once the wood is burning, damp down with a little water to create more smoke. Smoking wood is available in chips and chunks; chips burn quickly so should be added towards the end of the cooking process. Chunks should last through the entire cooking process.

If glazing meat, such as ham, and smoking together, always glaze before adding wood. (Note that some woods, such as pine or cedar produce acrid smoke and are unsuitable for cooking. Use only wood sold specifically for smoking.)

A barbecue flatplate can be used to stir-fry vegetables.

Fish is ready when the flesh has turned opaque and flakes back easily.

RARE, MEDIUM OR WELL-DONE?

Not everybody likes their steak, beef or lamb cooked for the same length of time. Test for 'doneness' by gently pressing the meat with tongs or a flat-bladed knife. If in doubt, remove it from the barbecue and make a small cut in the meat to check its colour.

Here is a guide to how the 5 classic degrees of 'doneness' should feel and look.

Medium-rare: Springy to touch, with moist, pale-red centre.

Bleu: Very soft to touch, red-raw inside, outer edge lightly cooked.

Medium: Firm to touch, pink in centre and crisp, brown edges.

Rare: Soft to touch, red centre, thin edge of cooked meat.

Well-done: Very firm to touch, brown outside and evenly cooked.

Alternatively, place butter in a piping bag and pipe individual servings over a piece of aluminium foil. Store, in refrigerator until required; place on food just before serving.

Always soften butter to room temperature before preparing.

GARLIC AND CHEESE BUTTER

Beat 100 g butter and 100 g softened cream cheese until light and creamy. Add 1 crushed garlic clove and 1 tablespoon each chopped fresh basil and chopped fresh parsley. Beat until smooth. Using plastic wrap, form into a log shape and refrigerate.

LIME AND CHILLI BUTTER

Beat 125 g butter until light and creamy. Add 1 tablespoon lime juice, 1 teaspoon grated lime rind, 1 teaspoon chopped chilli and 2 teaspoons chopped fresh coriander. Beat until smooth. Using plastic wrap, form into a log shape and refrigerate.

SAVOURY ANCHOVY BUTTER

Combine 200 g butter, 4 drained anchovy fillets, 2 chopped spring onions, 1 garlic clove and 1 tablespoon grated lemon rind in food processor bowl. Process 20–30 seconds or until mixture forms a smooth paste. Transfer to small serving pots and refrigerate.

CAPSICUM AND TOMATO BUTTER

Cut 1 large red capsicum in half; remove seeds and membrane. Brush skin with oil. Place under preheated grill 5–10 minutes or until skin blackens. Cover with damp cloth and stand 5 minutes. Remove skin from capsicum; discard. Chop flesh roughly. Combine capsicum, 200 g

FLAVOURED BUTTERS

Butters add an interesting touch to a meal and can be used instead of sauce. They are delicious on meat, chicken and seafood, as well as cooked vegetables or spread on hot bread.

Make 2 or 3 butters at a time and store, covered, in the refrigerator for up to 2 weeks. Butters can be frozen for several months. Shape butters into a log and slice off the required amount, then return to the fridge.

Shape flavoured butter into a log, freeze and slice rounds as required.

A piping bag and a variety of nozzles can make interesting shapes.

Serving pots can be stored in the refrigerator for several weeks.

chopped butter, 4 drained sun-dried tomatoes in oil and salt and pepper, to taste, in food processor bowl. Process 20–30 seconds or until smooth. Transfer to a serving bowl, cover in plastic wrap, and refrigerate.

MARINATING AND BASTING

Because food cooks quickly on the barbecue, some foods should be marinated beforehand. Marinate food, preferably overnight, but at least a few hours ahead in a non-metal dish, covered, in the refrigerator; turn meat in marinade occasionally. Vinegar, citrus juice or wine-based marinades are ideal for tougher meats as they tenderise the fibres of the meat.

Oil-based marinades moisturise meats and are suitable for meat such as chicken or pork. Yoghurt-based marinades are used with chicken or lamb, generally. The marinade will form a delicious crust over the meat when it is cooked.

Drain food from marinade and cook food as quickly as possible. If marinade is oil- or vinegar-based, reserve and use to baste.

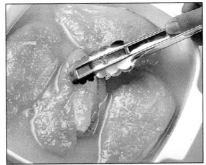
Meat should be turned once or twice during the marinating process.

BASTING

While not all foods need to be marinated before barbecuing, all should be basted during cooking. Basting seals moisture and prevents the food from sticking. Baste with olive oil or reserved marinade, lightly, on both sides. A pastry brush, or clean, unused paintbrush is ideal for this. Do not use a brush with plastic bristles as the plastic may melt onto the food.

PLANNING YOUR BARBECUE

Design your menu to take full advantage of the barbecue—vegetables,

kebabs, breads, even desserts can be cooked or warmed easily.

Serve at least 1 salad with the cooked food. Dressings and sauces can be made in advance and stored in a jar in the refrigerator. Assemble salads up to 1 day in advance, but dress just before serving.

Light the fire about an hour before you are planning to use it; check the fire occasionally; it can easily go out if unattended.

Assemble all necessary utensils and accessories (for example, tongs, forks, knives, plates and basting brushes) before cooking.

Have plenty of snacks and drinks available for your guests, but place them well away from the fire.

Have a hose or water bottle near by in case of emergencies. (As a general safety rule, do not attempt to barbecue in strong winds.) A torch may be useful if barbecuing at night.

Always extinguish a fire once you have finished cooking on it. If possible, clean out the barbecue as soon as it has cooled down; brush or scrape grills and flatplates, discard ash and embers.

INDIRECT COOKING

Indirect cooking roasts or bakes food more slowly than direct cooking. It also allows for adding fragrant wood chips to the coals which introduces extra flavour to the food.

To prepare a weber for indirect cooking:

1. Remove lid; open bottom vent.
2. Position bottom grill inside bowl and attach charcoal rails. Heap coals in rails and position firelighters inside coals.
3. Light fire and allow coals to develop to fine-ash stage. (Leave lid off while fire develops.) Place a drip-tray or baking dish on bottom grill. Position top grill; add food.

To prepare a weber for smoking:

1. Prepare barbecue as above.
2. When coals reach fine-ash stage, add wood chips; fill drip tray or baking dish with 4 cups hot water. Cover with lid until fragrant smoke develops.
3. Remove lid; centre food on top grill. Cover with lid.

Position two or three firelighters within the coals.

Light fire and allow the coals to develop.

Place a drip tray underneath top grill when coals are ready.

Spoon a generous quantity of smoking wood over hot coals.

BURGERS AND SAUSAGES

BEST-EVER BURGER WITH HOMEMADE BARBECUE SAUCE

Preparation time: 20 minutes
+ 30 minutes refrigeration
Total cooking time: 25 minutes
Serves 6

750 g beef mince
250 g sausage mince
1 small onion, finely chopped
1 tablespoon Worcestershire sauce
2 tablespoons tomato sauce
1 cup fresh breadcrumbs
1 egg, lightly beaten
2 large onions, extra, thinly sliced in rings
6 wholemeal rolls
6 small lettuce leaves
1 large tomato, sliced

HOMEMADE BARBECUE SAUCE

2 teaspoons oil
1 small onion, finely chopped
3 teaspoons brown vinegar
1 tablespoon soft brown sugar
1/3 cup tomato sauce
2 teaspoons Worcestershire sauce
2 teaspoons soy sauce

1 Place beef mince and sausage mince in a large bowl. Add onion, sauces, breadcrumbs and egg. Using hands, mix until thoroughly combined. Divide mixture into 6 equal portions and shape into 1.5 cm thick patties. Refrigerate patties for at least 30 minutes. Prepare and heat the barbecue.
2 Place patties on hot lightly oiled barbecue or flatplate. Barbecue over hottest part of fire 8 minutes each side, turning once. While patties are cooking, fry onions on oiled flatplate until golden.
To assemble burgers: Split rolls in half. Place bases on individual serving plates. Top each base with lettuce leaf, patty, tomato slice and fried onions. Top with a generous dollop of the Barbecue Sauce. Cover with remaining bun half.
3 For Homemade Barbecue Sauce, heat oil in a small pan. Cook onion 5 minutes or until soft. Add vinegar, sugar and sauces; stir to combine and bring to the boil. Reduce heat and simmer 3 minutes. Cool.

COOK'S FILE

Storage time: Burgers can be made up to 4 hours in advance; sauce can be made up to 1 week in advance. Store burgers and sauce in the refrigerator.

CHICKEN BURGER WITH TANGY GARLIC MAYONNAISE

Preparation time: 20 minutes
+ 3 hours marinating
Total cooking time: 15 minutes
Serves 4

4 chicken breast fillets
½ cup lime juice
1 tablespoon sweet chilli sauce
4 bacon rashers
4 hamburger buns
4 lettuce leaves
1 large tomato, sliced

GARLIC MAYONNAISE
2 egg yolks
2 cloves garlic, crushed
1 tablespoon Dijon mustard
1 tablespoon lemon juice
½ cup olive oil

1 Place chicken in a shallow non-metal dish; prick chicken breasts with a skewer several times. Combine lime juice and chilli sauce in a jug. Pour over chicken; cover. Marinate several hours or overnight. Prepare and light barbecue 1 hour before cooking. Remove and discard rind from bacon, cut bacon in half crossways.
2 Place chicken and bacon on hot lightly greased barbecue grill or flatplate. Cook bacon 5 minutes or until crisp. Cook chicken another 5–10 minutes until well browned and cooked through, turning once. Cut hamburger buns in half and toast each side until lightly browned. Top bases with lettuce, tomato, chicken and bacon. Top with Garlic Mayonnaise; finish with remaining bun top.
3 To make the Garlic Mayonnaise, place the egg yolks, garlic, mustard and lemon juice in a food processor bowl or blender. Process until smooth. With motor constantly running, add the oil in a thin, steady stream. Process until mayonnaise reaches a thick consistency. Cover mayonnaise and refrigerate until required.

COOK'S FILE
Storage time: Chicken can be marinated up to 1 day ahead. Store mayonnaise up to 1 month in refrigerator.

1

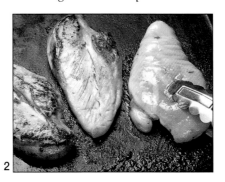

2

3

2 tomatoes, thinly sliced
6 large slices beetroot, drained
6 pineapple rings, drained
tomato sauce

1 Prepare and heat the barbecue, then place the mince, onion, egg, breadcrumbs, tomato paste, Worcestershire sauce, parsley, salt and pepper in large bowl. Mix with hands until well combined.

2 Divide mixture into 6 portions. Shape each portion into round patties 1.5 cm thick. Cover and set aside. Slice onions into thin rings. Heat butter on hot barbecue flatplate. Cook onions, turning often until well browned. Move onions towards outer edge of flatplate to keep warm. Brush barbecue grill or flatplate liberally with oil.

3 Cook meat patties 3–4 minutes each side or until browned and cooked through. Move patties to cooler part of barbecue or transfer to plate and keep warm. Place slice of cheese on each patty. (The heat of the burger will be enough to partially melt the cheese.) Heat a small amount of butter in a large frying pan. Fry eggs and bacon until eggs are cooked through and bacon is golden and crisp. Remove from heat. To assemble burgers: Place toasted bun bases on individual serving plates. Top each with lettuce, tomato, beetroot and pineapple. Place cooked meat patty on top, followed by cooked onions, egg, bacon and tomato sauce. Place remaining bun halves on top. Serve with potato chips, if desired.

COOK'S FILE

Storage time: Burgers can be prepared up to 4 hours in advance. Refrigerate until needed. Burger best prepared just before serving.

BURGER WITH THE WORKS

Preparation time: 40 minutes
Total cooking time: 10–15 minutes
Serves 6

750 g lean beef mince
1 onion, finely chopped
1 egg

½ cup fresh breadcrumbs
2 tablespoons tomato paste
1 tablespoon Worcestershire sauce
2 tablespoons chopped fresh parsley
salt and cracked pepper, to taste
3 large onions
30 g butter
6 slices cheddar cheese
6 eggs, extra
6 rashers bacon
6 large hamburger buns, lightly toasted
shredded lettuce

1

2

3

TURKEY BURGER WITH TARRAGON MAYONNAISE

Preparation time: 25 minutes
Total cooking time: 20 minutes
Serves 6

1 kg turkey mince
1 small onion, finely chopped
2 teaspoons lemon rind
2 tablespoons sour cream
1 cup fresh breadcrumbs
6 onion bread rolls

TARRAGON MAYONNAISE

1 egg yolk
1 tablespoon tarragon vinegar
½ teaspoon French mustard

1 cup olive oil
salt and white pepper, to taste

1 Prepare and heat the barbecue. Place turkey mince in a mixing bowl. Add onion, rind, sour cream and breadcrumbs. Using hands, mix until thoroughly combined. Divide mixture into 6 equal portions and shape into 1.5 cm thick patties.
2 Place patties on hot lightly oiled barbecue grill or flatplate. Cook 7 minutes each side, turning once. Serve on an onion roll with salad fillings and Tarragon Mayonnaise.
3 To make Tarragon Mayonnaise, place yolk, half the vinegar and the mustard in a small mixing bowl. Whisk together 1 minute until light and creamy. Add oil about 1 teaspoon at a time, whisking constantly until mixture thickens. Increase flow of oil to a thin stream; continue whisking until all the oil has been incorporated. Stir in remaining vinegar and salt and white pepper.

COOK'S FILE

Storage time: Burgers can be prepared up to 1 day in advance and mayonnaise up to 4 hours in advance. Store both in the refrigerator.
Variation: Mayonnaise can also be made in the food processor. Add the oil in a thin stream, with motor constantly running, until the mixture thickens and turns creamy.
Note: Do not use black pepper in mayonnaise as it will discolour the mixture.

1

2

3

VEGETARIAN BURGER WITH CORIANDER GARLIC CREAM

Preparation time: 30 minutes
Total cooking time: 20 minutes
Makes 10 burgers

1 cup red lentils
1 tablespoon oil
2 onions, sliced
1 tablespoon tandoori mix powder
425 g can chickpeas, drained
1 tablespoon grated fresh ginger
1 egg
1/4 cup chopped fresh parsley
2 tablespoons chopped fresh
    coriander
2 1/4 cups stale breadcrumbs
flour, for dusting

CORIANDER GARLIC CREAM

1/2 cup sour cream
1/2 cup cream
1 clove garlic, crushed
2 tablespoons chopped fresh
    coriander
2 tablespoons chopped
    fresh parsley

1 Prepare and heat the barbecue. Bring large pan of water to the boil. Add lentils to boiling water and simmer uncovered 8 minutes or until tender. Drain well. Heat oil in pan, cook onions until tender. Add tandoori mix; stir until fragrant; cook the mixture slightly.
2 Place the chickpeas, half the lentils, ginger, egg and onion mixture in food processor bowl. Process for 20 seconds or until smooth. Transfer the mixture to a bowl. Stir in the remaining lentils, parsley, coriander and breadcrumbs; combine well. Divide mixture into 10 portions.

3 Shape portions into round patties. (If mixture is too soft, refrigerate for 15 minutes or until firm.) Toss patties in flour. Shake off excess. Place patties on hot lightly greased barbecue grill or flatplate. Cook 3–4 minutes each side or until browned, turning once. Serve with Coriander Garlic Cream. To make the Garlic Cream, combine sour cream, cream, garlic and herbs in bowl; mix well.

COOK'S FILE
Storage time: Patties can be prepared up to 2 days ahead and stored, covered, in refrigerator. Cream can be made up to 3 days ahead. Store, covered, in refrigerator.
Note: This recipe can be served as a vegetarian dish on its own, or as an interesting accompaniment to other meat dishes. Coriander Cream is delicious with chicken or fish burgers.

HERB BURGER

Preparation time: 20 minutes
Total cooking time: 15–20 minutes
Makes 8 burgers

750 g minced beef or lamb
2 tablespoons chopped fresh basil
1 tablespoon chopped fresh chives
1 tablespoon chopped fresh rosemary
1 tablespoon chopped fresh thyme
2 tablespoons lemon juice
1 cup stale breadcrumbs
1 egg
pinch salt
pinch pepper
2 long crusty bread sticks
lettuce leaves
2 tomatoes, sliced
bottled tomato sauce

1 Prepare and heat the barbecue. Place mince in a bowl and combine with the herbs, juice, breadcrumbs, egg, salt and pepper. Mix with hands until well combined. Divide mixture into 8 portions.
2 Shape portions into thick rectangular patties about 15 cm long. Place on hot barbecue flatplate or grill. Cook 5–10 minutes each side until well browned and just cooked through.
3 Cut each bread stick into 4 sections. Cut each piece in half, horizontally. Top bases with lettuce, tomato, herb burger and tomato sauce. Finish with bread tops. Serve immediately.

COOK'S FILE

Storage time: Mince mixture can be made 1 day ahead. Refrigerate.

1

2

3

HONEY SOY SAUSAGES

Preparation time: 15 minutes
+ overnight marinating
Total cooking time: 5–6 minutes
Serves 4–6

8–10 thick beef or pork sausages
3 cm piece fresh ginger
⅓ cup honey
⅓ cup soy sauce
1 clove garlic, crushed
1 tablespoon sweet sherry
2 sprigs fresh thyme

1 Place the sausages in a large bowl or shallow non-metal dish. Peel ginger and grate finely. Combine honey, soy sauce, ginger, garlic, sherry and thyme in jug; mix well.
2 Pour marinade over sausages. Cover and refrigerate overnight to allow flavours to be absorbed.
3 Prepare and heat barbecue 1 hour before cooking. Lightly grease the barbecue grill or flatplate. Cook sausages 5–6 minutes, away from the hottest part of the fire, brushing occasionally with marinade. Turn sausages frequently to prevent marinade burning. (Marinade should form a thick, slightly sticky glaze around the sausages.) Serve with barbecued pineapple slices, if desired.

COOK'S FILE

Storage time: Sausages can be marinated up to 2 days in advance. Store in refrigerator.
Hints: Buy sausages made from pure beef or pork. They are tastier and less fatty than the cheaper variety.
Honey Soy Marinade can also be used over chicken, beef or lamb. Marinate overnight for best results.

LAMB BURGER WITH MANGO, CORIANDER AND MINT SALSA

Preparation time: 30 minutes
Total cooking time: 10–15 minutes
Makes 8 patties

425 g can mangoes
1 kg lamb mince
1 small red onion, finely chopped
1 tablespoon chopped fresh coriander
1 egg
1 cup stale breadcrumbs
2 tablespoons sweet chilli sauce
¼ teaspoon salt

MANGO SALSA
½ small red onion, chopped
1 tablespoon chopped fresh mint
1 tablespoon chopped fresh coriander leaves
⅓ cup finely chopped cucumber
1 tablespoon white wine vinegar
1 small red chilli, chopped
2 teaspoons sugar
salt and pepper to taste

1 Prepare and heat barbecue. Lightly grease the barbecue plate. Drain the mangoes, reserving 1 tablespoon of syrup. Cut mangoes into 1 cm cubes. Combine the mince, onion, bread-crumbs, coriander, egg, chilli sauce and salt in bowl. Add ¼ cup of the mango; mix until combined. Divide into 8 portions. Shape into patties.
2 Place patties on hot lightly oiled barbecue flatplate. Cook 5 minutes each side or until cooked through. Serve with Mango Salsa.
3 To make the Mango Salsa, mix the remaining mango and syrup with onion, herbs, cucumber, vinegar, chilli, sugar, salt and pepper in bowl.

COOK'S FILE
Storage time: Patties can be prepared a day ahead and stored, covered, in the refrigerator.
Hint: Salsa can also be served as a dip; mix through a little plain yoghurt and serve with chunks of fresh bread.

HERB AND GARLIC SAUSAGE WITH RED ONION RELISH

Preparation time: 20 minutes
Total cooking time: 40 minutes
Serves 4

4 herb and garlic sausages
25 cm square focaccia
4 lettuce leaves, shredded
1 medium tomato, sliced

RED ONION RELISH
2 tablespoons olive oil
2 medium red onions, sliced
2 teaspoons malt vinegar
1 tablespoon sugar

1 Prepare and heat barbecue. Place sausages on hot, lightly oiled barbecue grill or flatplate. Barbecue, turning frequently, 10 minutes or until well browned and cooked through. Cut sausages in half, lengthways.
2 Cut focaccia into quarters, split in half horizontally and toast under preheated grill each side until golden. Place lettuce and tomato on each focaccia base, followed by sausage.
Top with Red Onion Relish. Cover with remaining focaccia squares. Serve with grilled peppers, if desired.
3 To make Red Onion Relish, heat oil in medium pan, cook onions over medium-low heat 15 minutes, stirring frequently, until very soft but not browned. Add vinegar and sugar; cook a further 10 minutes. Serve warm or at room temperature.

COOK'S FILE
Storage time: Relish can be made up to 1 day in advance.
Hint: Use any of the wide variety of flavoured sausages now available from butchers or some supermarkets.

Lamb Burger with Mango, Coriander and Mint Salsa (top) and Herb and Garlic Sausage with Red Onion Relish.

BREAKFAST SKEWERS WITH QUICK TOMATO SAUCE

Preparation time: 25 minutes
Total cooking time: 35 minutes
Serves 4

4 beef sausages
16 small button mushrooms
4 rashers bacon
4 lamb kidneys
30 g butter, melted
4 large tomatoes, halved

QUICK TOMATO SAUCE
1 tablespoon oil
1 small onion, finely chopped
3 medium tomatoes, peeled, finely
   chopped
¼ cup barbecue sauce

1 Prepare and heat the barbecue.
Place sausages in a large pan, cover
with cold water and bring slowly to
simmering point. Leave to cool. Drain
well and cut each sausage into six
pieces.
2 Wipe mushrooms clean with paper
towels. Chop bacon into bite-size
pieces. Trim kidneys, remove core
and cut into quarters.
3 Thread sausage, bacon, kidney and
mushrooms alternately on skewers.
Place skewers on hot lightly oiled
barbecue flatplate, brush with melted
butter and cook 15 minutes, turning
occasionally, or until browned and
cooked through. Place tomatoes on
hot grill cut-side down; cook for
5 minutes. Serve skewers with
tomatoes and Quick Tomato Sauce.
4 To make Quick Tomato Sauce, heat
oil in a small pan. Cook onion over
medium-low heat 5 minutes until
soft; add tomatoes and sauce. Cook
10 minutes, stirring occasionally.
Serve warm or at room temperature.

COOK'S FILE

Storage time: Sauce can be made up
to 1 day in advance.
Hints: If using wooden skewers, soak
in cold water 1 hour before assembling.
This will help to prevent the wood
burning during cooking. Serve this dish
with scrambled eggs and wholemeal
English muffins for a hearty breakfast.

MUSTARD BURGER WITH TOMATO AND ONION SALAD

Preparation time: 20 minutes
Total cooking time: 10 minutes
Makes 8 patties

1 kg beef mince
¼ cup seeded mustard
2 teaspoons Dijon mustard
1 teaspoon beef stock powder
1 cup stale breadcrumbs
1 egg
1 teaspoon black pepper

¼ cup chopped red capsicum

TOMATO AND ONION SALAD

1 small red onion
4 tomatoes
2 tablespoons red wine vinegar
1½ teaspoons caster sugar
2 teaspoons lemon juice

1 Place beef mince in large bowl. Add mustards, stock powder, breadcrumbs, egg, pepper and capsicum; mix well with hands. Divide the mixture into 8 portions.
2 Shape portions into round patties. Cook on hot lightly greased barbecue grill or flatplate 2–3 minutes each

side, turning once. Serve with Tomato and Onion Salad and bread of choice.
3 To make Tomato and Onion Salad, chop onion and tomatoes into small cubes. Combine in bowl with vinegar, sugar and juice; mix well.

COOK'S FILE

Storage time: Patties can be prepared 1 day ahead. Cover and store in refrigerator and barbecue just before serving. Salad can be made 1 day ahead. Store, covered, in refrigerator.
Hint: Substitute any mustard for Dijon. German or American mustard makes a mild-tasting burger. English mustard makes a hotter-tasting burger.

CRACKED WHEAT AND LAMB BURGER

Preparation time: 25 minutes
+ 30 minutes standing
Total cooking time: 5–10 minutes
Serves 4

¼ cup (45 g/1½ oz) cracked wheat
   (burghul)
400 g (12⅔ oz) lean lamb mince
1 tablespoon lime juice
2 teaspoons grated lime rind
3 cloves garlic, crushed

⅓ cup (20 g/⅔ oz) finely chopped
   fresh parsley
4 tablespoons chopped fresh mint
2–3 tablespoons oil
1 large red onion, finely chopped
1 large tomato, finely chopped
1 teaspoon soft brown sugar
4 bread rolls
salad leaves and plain yoghurt,
   for serving

1 Soak the wheat in ¼ cup (60 ml/ 2 fl oz) water for 30 minutes. Drain and squeeze out the excess water. Using your hands, mix together the wheat, lamb mince, lime juice and

rind, 2 cloves of garlic, parsley, 2 tablespoons of mint and plenty of salt and freshly ground black pepper. Divide the mixture into 4; shape into patties.
2 Prepare and heat the barbecue. Lightly oil barbecue plate and cook the patties for 3–4 minutes each side, or until brown and cooked through.
3 Mix the onion, tomato, remaining garlic and mint, brown sugar and some salt and black pepper in a bowl. Fill the rolls with the salad leaves, a patty, some of the onion and tomato mixture and a spoonful of yoghurt.

Soak the cracked wheat in water for about 30 minutes, to soften.

Divide the mixture into 4 and shape into patties.

Mix together the onion, tomato, garlic, mint, sugar, salt and pepper.

BARBECUED TUNA BURGER

Preparation time: 15 minutes
+ 2 hours refrigeration
Total cooking time: 10 minutes
Serves 4

700 g (1 lb 6⅔ oz) fresh tuna
3 spring onions, finely
   chopped
1 tablespoon mirin

1 teaspoon soy sauce
1 tablespoon lime juice

1 Finely chop the tuna until it resembles mince. Mix in a bowl with the spring onion, mirin, soy sauce and lime juice.
2 Divide the mixture into 4 and shape into round patties. Cover and refrigerate for 2 hours.
3 Cook patties on a preheated barbecue or chargrill pan for 8–10 minutes, or until cooked through, turning once. Serve hot or cold with

wedges of lime, your favourite relish and salad leaves.

COOK'S FILE

Note: This recipe can also be used to make tiny tuna balls to serve with drinks. With wet hands, shape heaped tablespoons of the mixture into balls. Refrigerate for 2 hours. Preheat the oven to 180°C (350°F/Gas 4). Add a little oil to a large non-stick frying pan and cook in batches for 3 minutes, or until just brown. Transfer to a non-stick baking tray and bake in oven for 5 minutes.

Use a large, sharp knife to chop the tuna until it resembles mince.

Place the tuna patties on a plate, cover with plastic wrap and refrigerate.

Cook the patties for 8–10 minutes, or until cooked through. Turn them once.

Cracked Wheat and Lamb Burger (top) and Barbecued tuna Burger

CHEESY BURGERS WITH RED SALSA

Preparation time: 25 minutes
+ 1 hour standing
Total cooking time: 20 minutes
Serves 6

1 kg beef mince
1 small onion, finely chopped
2 tablespoons chopped
    fresh parsley
1 teaspoon dried oregano
1 tablespoon tomato paste
70 g cheddar cheese
6 white bread rolls
lettuce leaves

RED SALSA
2 medium red capsicum
1 medium ripe tomato, finely chopped
1 small red onion, finely chopped
1 tablespoon olive oil
2 teaspoons red wine vinegar

1 Prepare and heat the barbecue. Place mince in large mixing bowl; add onion, herbs and tomato paste. Using hands, mix until thoroughly combined. Divide mixture into 6 equal portions and shape into patties. Cut cheese into small squares. Make a cavity in the top of each patty with thumb. Place cheese in cavity and smooth mince over to enclose the cheese completely.
2 Place patties on hot lightly oiled barbecue grill or flatplate. Barbecue 4–5 minutes each side, turning once. Remove from barbecue; keep warm. Split each roll in half; place a lettuce leaf on the base of each, top with pattie and Red Salsa.
3 To make Red Salsa, trim the capsicum and remove all the seeds and membrane. Cut into wide pieces and place skin-side up under a hot grill. Cook 4–5 minutes or until skin blisters and blackens. Cover with damp tea-towel and leave to cook. Remove skin from capsicum and finely chop flesh. Combine with tomato, onion, olive oil and vinegar and stand at least 1 hour to allow flavours to develop. Serve the salsa at room temperature.

COOK'S FILE
Storage time: Burgers can be prepared up to 4 hours in advance. Salsa can be made up to 1 day in advance. Store, covered, in refrigerator.
Variation: camembert, brie or blue cheese can be used to stuff patties, if desired. Substitute bottled tomato sauce or ready-made salsa, available from supermarkets, if time is short.

1

2

3

BARBECUE CHILLI BEEF BURGERS

Preparation time: 25 minutes
+ 2 hours marinating
Cooking time: 8 minutes
Makes 18

1 kg beef mince
3 medium onions, grated
¼ cup finely chopped
   fresh parsley
1½ cups (135g) packaged
   breadcrumbs
1 egg, lightly beaten
1 tablespoon milk

1 tablespoon malt vinegar
1 tablespoon tomato paste
1 tablespoon chilli sauce
3 teaspoons dried oregano
   leaves

MUSTARD BUTTER
125g butter, softened
2 tablespoons soured cream
2 tablespoons German mustard

1 Prepare and heat the barbecue. Place mince in large mixing bowl; add onion, parsley, breadcrumbs, egg, milk, vinegar, tomato paste, sauces and oregano leaves. Mix well. Store in the refrigerator, covered with plastic wrap for 2 hours.

2 Divide the mixture into 18 even-sized portions. Shape each portion into a burger about 1.5 cm thick
3 Place burgers on a lightly oiled barbecue grill or flatplate. Cook over a high heat for 4 minutes each side or until well browned and cooked through. Serve the burgers with salad and dollops of Mustard Butter.
4 To make Mustard Butter, beat the butter, sour cream and mustard in a small bowl for 2 minutes or until well combined. Leave the mixture uncovered for 20 minutes to allow flavours to blend.

BARBECUED HOT DOGS WITH CREAMY SLAW

Preparation time: 20 minutes
Total cooking time: 10 minutes
Serves 6

6 large thick, spicy frankfurts
1 tablespoon oil
6 hot dog rolls
6 small lettuce leaves

CREAMY SLAW
100 g red cabbage
100 g green cabbage
2 spring onions
½ cup whole egg mayonnaise
1 tablespoon German mustard

1 Prepare and heat the barbecue. Make 4 diagonal cuts in each frankfurt, slicing halfway through. Brush frankfurts with oil, and cook on hot lightly oiled barbecue flatplate 7–10 minutes or until cooked through.

2 Split rolls lengthways through the centre top; line with lettuce leaf. Place Creamy Slaw on lettuce, and top with hot dog. Serve immediately.
3 To make Creamy Slaw, finely shred cabbage; finely chop spring onions. Combine mayonnaise with mustard. Place all ingredients in a mixing bowl and toss to combine thoroughly.

COOK'S FILE

Storage time: Slaw can be made up to 4 hours in advance. Barbecue frankfurts just before serving.

1

2

3

PORK SAUSAGE BURGER WITH MUSTARD CREAM

Preparation time: 20 minutes
Total cooking time: 15 minutes
Serves 6

1 kg pork mince
1 small onion, finely chopped
1 cup fresh breadcrumbs
2 cloves garlic, crushed
1 egg, lightly beaten
1 teaspoon dried sage
6 long crusty bread rolls

MUSTARD CREAM
½ cup sour cream
1 tablespoon wholegrain mustard
2 teaspoons lemon juice

1 Prepare and heat the barbecue. Place mince in large mixing bowl. Add onion, breadcrumbs, garlic, egg and sage. Using hands, mix to combine thoroughly. Divide the mixture into 6 equal portions, shape into sausage shapes about 16 cm long.

2 Place burgers on hot, lightly oiled barbecue flatplate or grill. Barbecue 5–10 minutes, turning occasionally. Place on a long crusty roll with Mustard Cream. Garnish with chives and serve with a salad, if desired.

3 To make Mustard Cream, place sour cream, mustard and juice in a small bowl and stir to combine.

COOK'S FILE

Storage time: Burgers can be prepared up to 4 hours in advance.

MARINADES FOR SAUSAGES

Sausages now come in a range of gourmet flavours—from sun-dried tomato to spicy lamb. These sausages need no enhancement, just cook and serve with a salad or some vegetables. But for creative cooks who want their trad-itional beef or pork sausages to take pride of place on their barbecue menu, a simple baste or marinade can transform an ordinary sausage into something extra special.

Marinades add flavour, and when they contain an acid ingredient like lemon juice, wine or vinegar, they also tenderize the meat. Marinate sausages for several hours or overnight to allow them to absorb the flavours.

Similar to a marinade, bastes are brushed over the food while it cooks, to give a lovely, subtle flavour. Basting also keeps sausages moist while they cook .

The following recipes make marinade for about 12 sausages. To use as a baste, brush the mixture over the sausages while they are cooking, rather than marinating them first.

FRESH HERB MARINADE

Mix the following ingredients thoroughly in a bowl: ¼ cup (60 ml/2 fl oz) olive oil, 2–3 tablespoons lemon juice or balsamic vinegar, 1–2 crushed cloves garlic, 3 teaspoons soft brown sugar, some salt and freshly ground black pepper and 4 tablespoons of chopped fresh mixed herbs (use any combination you wish—chives, lemon thyme, rosemary, parsley, basil, coriander, mint, oregano or marjoram). Prick the sausages all over and marinate, covered, for at least 3 hours or overnight in the refrigerator. Turn the sausages occasionally. Use with any type of sausage. This mixture is also suitable for basting.

HONEY AND CHILLI MARINADE

Mix the following ingredients thoroughly in a bowl: ¼ cup (60 ml/2 fl oz) soy sauce,

1 tablespoon grated fresh ginger, 2 teaspoons grated lemon rind, ¼ cup (90 g/3 oz) honey, 1–2 crushed cloves garlic, 1 tablespoon sherry or rice wine and 3 tablespoons sweet chilli sauce. Prick the sausages all over and marinate, covered, for at least 3 hours or overnight in the refrigerator. Turn the sausages occasionally. This marinade goes well with any kind of sausage. It is also suitable for basting.

SPICY TANDOORI MARINADE

Mix the following ingredients thoroughly in a bowl: 1 tablespoon oil, 2 teaspoons each of ground cumin, coriander and paprika, 3 teaspoons turmeric, 2 teaspoons each of fresh grated ginger and tamarind sauce, 2 crushed cloves garlic, ½–1 teaspoon chilli powder, ½ teaspoon salt, 3 tablespoons tomato sauce and 200 g (6½ oz)

plain yoghurt. Prick the sausages all over and marinate, covered, for at least 3 hours or overnight in the refrigerator. Turn the sausages occasionally. Use for lamb or chicken sausages. This mixture is also suitable for basting.

Note: You can use a commercial tandoori paste or powder if you prefer.

PLUM AND CORIANDER MARINADE

Mix the following ingredients thoroughly in a bowl: ¼ cup (60 ml/2 fl oz) plum sauce, 1–2 crushed cloves garlic,1 tablespoon each of Worcestershire and soy sauce, 2 tablespoons each of lime juice and chopped fresh coriander and ¼ cup (60 ml/2 fl oz) tomato sauce. Prick the sausages all over and marinate, covered, for at least 3 hours or overnight in the refrigerator. Turn the sausages

occasionally. This mixture is also suitable for basting.

APRICOT AND ONION MARINADE

Mix the following ingredients thoroughly in a bowl: ⅓ cup (80 ml/2¾ fl oz) apricot nectar, 3 tablespoons lime marmalade, 2 crushed cloves garlic, 2 tablespoons olive oil, 1–2 tablespoons French onion soup mix, 1 tablespoon chopped fresh chives, a dash of Worcestershire sauce. Prick the sausages all over and marinate, covered, for at least 3 hours or overnight in the refrigerator. Turn the sausages occasionally. This mixture is also suitable for basting.

Marinades, clockwise, from top left: Fresh Herb; Honey and Chilli; Spicy Tandoori; Plum and Coriander; Apricot and Onion

BEEF, LAMB AND PORK

TANGY BEEF RIBS

Preparation time: 20 minutes
+ 3 hours marinating
Total cooking time: 15–20 minutes
Serves 4

1 kg beef ribs
½ cup tomato sauce
2 tablespoons Worcestershire sauce
2 tablespoons soft brown sugar
1 teaspoon paprika
¼ teaspoon chilli powder
1 clove garlic, crushed

1 Chop the ribs into individual serving pieces, if necessary. Bring a large pan of water to boil. Cook the ribs in boiling water for 5 minutes; drain.
2 Combine the tomato sauce, Worcestershire sauce, sugar, paprika, chilli powder and garlic in large bowl and mix well. Add ribs to sauce. Cover and marinate, in refrigerator, several hours or overnight. Prepare and heat barbecue 1 hour before cooking.
3 Cook ribs on hot lightly greased barbecue grill or flatplate for 10–15 minutes, brushing frequently with marinade, or until ribs are well browned and cooked through. Serve with favourite barbecued vegetables or slices of grilled fresh pineapple, if desired.

COOK'S FILE
Storage time: Ribs are best cooked just before serving.
Hint: If time is short combine the ribs with the marinade and leave at room temperature, covered, for up to 2 hours. The meat will absorb the flavours of the marinade more quickly at room temperature. (This principle applies to all marinades.)
Note: Ribs can be bought as a long piece or cut into individual pieces. If chopping ribs yourself, you will need to use a sharp cleaver. Alternatively, ribs can be cooked in one piece and chopped into pieces after cooking, when the bone is softer. A longer cooking time is required if cooked as a single piece.
Pork ribs can also be used in this recipe. Use either the thick, meaty ribs, which are like beef ribs, or the long thin spare ribs (also known as American-style ribs). Pork spare ribs have less meat so need less cooking time. The ribs are excellent for picnics as they are easily eaten with the fingers.
Veal ribs are extremely tender and are sometimes available from speciality butchers.

1

2

3

BARBECUED STEAK WITH CARAMELISED BALSAMIC ONIONS AND MUSTARD CREME FRAICHE

Preparation time: 15 minutes
Cooking time: 35 minutes
Serves 4

1½ tablespoons wholegrain mustard
200 g crème fraîche
2 capsicums (1 red and 1 yellow), seeded and quartered
2 zucchini, trimmed and sliced lengthways into strips
2 tablespoons oil
2 large red onions, thinly sliced
4 rump steaks (about 200 g each)
2 tablespoons soft brown sugar
¼ cup (60 ml) balsamic vinegar

1 Heat your barbecue or preheat a large chargrill pan to hot. Combine the mustard and crème fraîche in a bowl. Season. Then cover and set aside.

2 Brush the capsicum and zucchini with 1 tablespoon of the oil. Cook the capsicum, turning regularly, on the barbecue for 5 minutes, or until tender and slightly charred. Remove and cover with foil. Repeat with the zucchini, also cooking for 5 minutes.

3 Heat the remaining oil on the barbecue, then cook the onion, turning occasionally, for 5–10 minutes, or until softened. When nearly soft, push to the side of the barbecue, then add the steaks and cook on each side for 3–4 minutes (medium-rare), or until cooked to your liking. Remove the steaks, cover them with foil and allow to rest. Spread the onion over the barbecue once again, reduce the heat, sprinkle with sugar and cook for 1–2 minutes, or until the sugar has dissolved and the onion appear glossy. Add the vinegar, stirring continuously for 1–2 minutes, or until it is compeltely absorbed. Remove at once.

4 Peel the skin off the capsicum, then divide among four serving plates with the zucchini. Place the steaks on top, season and top with the balsamic onions. Serve with the mustard crème fraîche and a mixed leaf salad.

HOT PEPPERED STEAKS WITH HORSERADISH SAUCE

Preparation time: 15 minutes
Total cooking time: 10 minutes
Serves 4

4 (800 g) medium-sized sirloin steaks
¼ cup seasoned, cracked
   pepper

HORSERADISH SAUCE

2 tablespoons brandy
¼ cup beef stock
⅓ cup cream
1 tablespoon horseradish
   cream
½ teaspoon sugar
salt and pepper, to taste

1 Lightly grease then heat barbecue grill. Trim meat of excess fat and sinew. Coat steaks on both sides with pepper, pressing it firmly into the meat.

2 Barbecue steaks 5–10 minutes until cooked as desired. Serve with Horseradish Sauce and steamed vegetables, such as snow peas.
3 To make the Sauce, combine brandy and stock in pan. Bring to boil, reduce heat. Stir in cream, horseradish and sugar; stir until heated through. Season to taste.

COOK'S FILE

Storage time: Steaks best cooked close to serving.

FILLET STEAK WITH FLAVOURED BUTTERS

Preparation time: 30 minutes
Total cooking time: 15 minutes
Serves 4

4 fillet steaks (500 g)

GARLIC BUTTER
125 g butter
3 cloves garlic, crushed
2 spring onions, finely
   chopped

CAPSICUM AND HERB BUTTER
1 small red capsicum
125 g butter
2 teaspoons chopped fresh oregano
2 teaspoons chopped fresh chives
salt and pepper, to taste

1 Lightly grease and heat the barbecue plate. Trim steaks of excess fat and sinew. Using a sharp knife, cut a pocket in side of each steak. To make Garlic Butter, beat butter in bowl until creamy, add garlic and chopped spring onions; beat until smooth. To make Capsicum & Herb Butter, cut capsicum in half. Remove seeds and membrane. Place cut-side down on cold grill tray. Brush skin with oil. Cook under preheated hot grill until skin blisters and blackens. Remove from grill. Cover with damp tea towel. Cool. Peel away skin and discard. Finely chop capsicum flesh. Beat butter until creamy. Add capsicum, herbs, salt and pepper; beat until smooth.
2 Push 2–3 teaspoons Garlic Butter into two of the steaks; push 2–3 teaspoons Capsicum and Herb Butter into remaining steaks.

3 Cook on hot barbecue grill or flatplate 4–5 minutes each side, turning once. Brush steaks frequently with any remaining flavoured butter while cooking.

COOK'S FILE
Storage time: Prepare steak 1 day ahead and store in refrigerator. Butters will keep 2 weeks in refrigerator, provided they are well covered.

BEEF TERIYAKI WITH CUCUMBER SALAD

Preparation time: 20 minutes
+ 30 minutes refrigeration
+ 10 minutes resting
Total cooking time: 20 minutes
Serves 4

4 scotch fillet steaks
1/3 cup (80 ml) soy sauce
2 tablespoons mirin
1 tablespoon sake (optional)
1 clove garlic, crushed
1 teaspoon grated fresh ginger
1 teaspoon sugar
1 teaspoon toasted sesame seeds

CUCUMBER SALAD
1 large Lebanese cucumber, peeled,
   seeded and diced
1/2 red capsicum, diced
2 spring onions, sliced thinly on
   the diagonal
2 teaspoons sugar
1 tablespoon rice wine vinegar

1 Place the steaks in a non-metallic dish. Combine the soy, mirin, sake, garlic and ginger and pour over the steaks. Cover with plastic wrap and refrigerate for at least 30 minutes.
2 To make the cucumber salad, place the cucumber, capsicum and spring onion in a small bowl. Place the sugar, rice wine vinegar and 1/4 cup (60 ml) water in a small saucepan and stir over medium heat until the sugar dissolves. Increase the heat and simmer rapidly for 3–4 minutes, or until slightly thickened. Pour over the cucumber salad, stir to combine and leave to cool completely.
3 Spray the barbecue grill or hot plate with oil spray and heat until very hot. Drain the steaks and reserve the marinade. Cook for 3–4 minutes on each side, or until cooked to your liking. Remove and rest the meat for 5–10 minutes before slicing.
4 Meanwhile, place the sugar and the reserved marinade in a small saucepan and heat, stirring, until the sugar has dissolved. Bring to the boil, then simmer for 2–3 minutes, remove from the heat and keep warm.
5 Slice each steak into 1 cm strips, being careful to keep the steak in its shape. Arrange the steak on each plate. Spoon on some of the marinade, a spoonful of cucumber salad and garnish with sesame seeds. Serve with steamed rice and the remaining cucumber salad.

Combine the cucumber, capsicum and spring onion with the dressing.

Cook the steaks for 3–4 minutes on each side, or until cooked to your liking.

THAI MEATBALL SKEWERS

Preparation time: 25 minutes
Total cooking time: 10 minutes
Serves 4

350 g beef mince
3 French shallots, finely chopped
3 cloves garlic, chopped
3 cm piece ginger, grated
1 tablespoon green or pink
  peppercorns, crushed
2 teaspoons Golden Mountain sauce

2 teaspoons fish sauce
2 teaspoons soft brown sugar
1/2 cup fresh coriander leaves
lime wedges
1 cucumber, chopped
3 sliced red or green chillies

1 Chop the mince with a cleaver or a large knife until the mince is very fine. Place the mince, French shallots, garlic, ginger, peppercorns, Golden Mountain sauce, fish sauce and the brown sugar in a bowl. Mix the ingredients until well combined.
2 Using 2 teaspoons of mixture at a time, form into balls. Thread the balls onto the bamboo skewers, using three balls for each skewer.
3 Place the skewers on an oiled grill plate or barbecue. Cook, turning frequently, for 7–8 minutes or until the meat is cooked through. Sprinkle with coriander. Serve skewers with the lime wedges, cucumber and sliced chillies.

COOK'S FILE

Hint: Soak the wooden skewers in water for at least 30 minutes before use, to help prevent them burning.
Variation: Pork mince, chicken mince or a combination may be used.

Use a large, sharp knife or a cleaver to chop the mince finely.

Form 2 teaspoonsful of mixture at a time into small, compact balls.

Cook the skewered meat balls, turning frequently, for 7–8 minutes.

INDIAN SEEKH KEBABS

Preparation time: 40 minutes
Total cooking time: 12 minutes
Serves 4

pinch of ground cloves
pinch of ground nutmeg
½ teaspoon chilli powder
1 teaspoon ground cumin
2 teaspoons ground coriander
3 cloves garlic, finely chopped
5 cm (2 inch) piece of fresh ginger,
    grated
500 g (1 lb) lean beef mince
1 tablespoon oil
2 tablespoons lemon juice

ONION AND MINT RELISH
1 red onion, finely chopped
1 tablespoon white vinegar
1 tablespoon lemon juice
1 tablespoon chopped fresh mint

1 Soak 12 thick wooden skewers in cold water for 15 minutes. Dry-fry the cloves, nutmeg, chilli, cumin and coriander in a heavy-based frying pan, over low heat, for about 2 minutes, shaking the pan constantly. Transfer to a bowl with the garlic and ginger and set aside.
2 Knead the mince firmly using your fingertips and base of your hand, for about 3 minutes, or until it becomes soft and a sticky (this process makes the meat tender when cooked). Add the mince to the spice and garlic mixture, add plenty of seasoning and mix well.
3 Form tablespoons of the meat into small, round patty shapes. Wet your hands and press 2 portions of the meat around a skewer, leaving a gap of

about 3 cm (1¼ inches) at the top of the skewer. Smooth the outside gently, place on baking paper and refrigerate while making the remaining kebabs.
4 To make Onion and Mint Relish, combine the onion, vinegar and lemon juice in a small bowl; refrigerate for 10 minutes. Stir in the mint

and season with pepper, to taste, just before serving.
5 Brush a preheated barbecue or hotplate with the oil. Grill the skewers for about 8 minutes, turning regularly and sprinkling with a little lemon juice. Serve the seekh kebabs with steamed rice and the Onion and Mint Relish.

Use a sharp knife to finely chop the cloves of garlic.

Dry-fry the spices in a heavy-based pan.

Press two rounds of meat around each wooden skewer.

LAMB CUTLETS WITH ROSEMARY MARINADE

Preparation time: 15 minutes
+ 20 minutes marinating
Total cooking time: 6–8 minutes
Serves 4

12 lamb cutlets
2 tablespoons chopped fresh
    rosemary
¼ cup olive oil
1½ teaspoons cracked black pepper
1 bunch fresh rosemary, extra

1 Prepare and heat the barbecue.
Trim cutlets of excess fat and sinew.
Place cutlets in shallow, non-metal
dish and brush with oil.
2 Scatter half the chopped rosemary
and pepper on meat; set aside for
20 minutes. Turn meat over and
brush with remaining oil, scatter
over remaining rosemary and pepper.
Tie the extra bunch of rosemary to
the handle of a wooden spoon.
3 Arrange cutlets on hot lightly
greased grill. Cook 2–3 minutes each
side. As cutlets cook, bat frequently
with the rosemary spoon. This will
release flavoursome oils into the
cutlets. When cutlets are almost
done, remove rosemary from the
spoon and drop it on the fire where it
will flare up briefly and infuse
rosemary smoke into the cutlets. Serve
with barbecued lemon slices, if desired.

COOK'S FILE

Storage time: Cook cutlets just before
serving.
Variation: This dish is ideal for a
barbecue picnic. Marinate and pack in a
sealed container with rosemary sprigs.
Add sprigs to the fire, as described
above.

LAMB PITTAS WITH FRESH MINT SALAD

Preparation time: 20 minutes
+ 30 minutes refrigeration
Total cooking time: 15 minutes
Serves 4

1 kg lean minced lamb
1 cup (60 g) finely chopped fresh parsley
½ cup (25 g) finely chopped fresh mint
1 onion, finely chopped
1 clove garlic, crushed
1 egg
1 teaspoon chilli sauce
4 small wholemeal pitta pockets

MINT SALAD
3 small vine-ripened tomatoes
1 small red onion, finely sliced
1 cup (20 g) fresh mint
1 tablespoon olive oil
2 tablespoons lemon juice

1 Place the lamb, parsley, mint, onion, garlic, egg and chilli sauce in a large bowl and mix together. Shape into eight small patties. Chill for 30 minutes. Preheat the oven to warm 160°C (315°F/Gas 2–3).
2 To make the Mint Salad, slice the tomatoes into thin rings and place in a bowl with the onion, mint, olive oil and lemon juice. Season well with salt and pepper. Gently toss to coat.
3 Wrap the pitta breads in foil and warm in the oven for 5–10 minutes.

4 Heat a barbecue chargrill or hot plate and brush with a little oil. When very hot, cook the patties for 3 minutes on each side. Do not turn until a nice crust has formed on the base or they will fall apart.
5 Remove the pitta breads from the oven. Cut the pockets in half, fill each half with some mint salad and a lamb patty. Serve with some low-fat yoghurt, if desired.

Mix the lamb, herbs, onion, garlic, egg and chilli sauce together with your hands.

Toss together the tomato and onion slices, mint, oil and lemon juice.

Chargrill the patties on a lightly oiled surface until a crust has formed.

LAMB CHOPS WITH PINEAPPLE SALSA

Preparation time: 20 minutes
Total cooking time: 10 minutes
Serves 6

12 lamb loin chops
2 tablespoons oil
1 teaspoon cracked black pepper

PINEAPPLE SALSA
½ ripe pineapple (or 400 g drained
    canned pineapple)
1 large red onion

1 fresh red chilli
1 tablespoon cider or rice vinegar
1 teaspoon sugar
salt and black pepper, to taste
2 tablespoons chopped mint

1 Prepare and heat the barbecue. Trim meat of excess fat and sinew. Brush chops with oil and season with pepper.
2 To make Pineapple Salsa, peel pineapple; remove core and eyes. Cut into 1 cm cubes. Peel onion, finely chop. Slit open chilli, scrape out seeds. Chop chilli flesh finely. Combine pineapple, onion and chilli in medium bowl; mix lightly.

Add vinegar, sugar, salt, pepper and mint; mix well.
3 Place lamb chops on lightly greased barbecue grill or flatplate. Cook chops 2–3 minutes each side, turning once, until just tender. Serve with Pineapple Salsa, baked potatoes and green salad, if desired.

COOK'S FILE

Storage: Chops are best barbecued just before serving. Salsa can be made 1 day in advance and refrigerated. Add herbs just before serving. (Red onion may affect colour of pineapple.)
Hint: Pineapple Salsa will also complement grilled tuna or salmon.

2

LAMB SOUVLAKE

Preparation time: 20 minutes
+ overnight marinating
+ 30 minutes standing
Total cooking time: 10 minutes
Serves 4

1 kg boned leg lamb, trimmed, cut
   into 2 cm cubes
¼ cup (60 ml) olive oil
2 teaspoons finely grated lemon rind
⅓ cup (80 ml) lemon juice
2 teaspoons dried oregano
½ cup (125 ml) dry white wine
2 large cloves garlic, finely chopped
2 fresh bay leaves
1 cup (250 g) Greek-style plain yoghurt
2 cloves garlic, crushed, extra

1 Place the lamb in a non-metallic bowl with 2 tablespoons of the olive oil, the lemon rind and juice, oregano, wine, garlic and bay leaves. Season with black pepper and toss to coat. Cover and refrigerate overnight.
2 Place the yoghurt and extra garlic in a bowl, mix together well and leave for 30 minutes.
3 Drain the lamb and pat dry. Thread onto 8 skewers and cook on a barbecue or chargrill plate, brushing with the remaining oil, for 7–8 minutes, or until brown on the outside and still a little rare in the middle. Drizzle with the garlic yoghurt and serve with warm pitta bread and a salad.

COOK'S FILE
Note: If using wooden skewers, soak them in water for 30 minutes to prevent burning during cooking.

Toss the lamb to coat well with the spicy marinade.

Pat the drained lamb dry and thread onto eight skewers.

Brush the remaining oil over the lamb skewers during cooking.

LAMB KOFTA KEBABS WITH TAHINI DRESSING

Preparation time: 25 minutes
Total cooking time: 10 minutes
Serves 4–6

600 g lean lamb
1 medium onion, roughly chopped
2 cloves garlic, roughly chopped
1 teaspoon cracked black pepper
1½ teaspoons ground cumin
½ teaspoon ground cinnamon
1 teaspoon sweet paprika
1 teaspoon salt
2 slices bread, crusts removed,
   quartered
1 egg, lightly beaten
olive oil, for coating

TAHINI DRESSING

2 tablespoons tahini (sesame paste)
3 teaspoons lemon juice
1 small garlic clove, crushed
pinch of salt
2–3 tablespoons water
2 tablespoons sour cream
1 tablespoon chopped fresh parsley

1 Trim meat of any excess fat and sinew. Cut into small pieces suitable for processing. Place lamb, onion, garlic, pepper, cumin, cinnamon, paprika, salt, bread and egg in food processor bowl. Process 20–30 seconds or until mixture becomes a smooth paste.

2 Divide mixture into 12. Using oil-coated hands, shape portions into sausages. Wrap sausages around skewers; cover and refrigerate until needed.

To make the Tahini Dressing, combine tahini, lemon juice, garlic, salt, water, sour cream and parsley in small bowl. Stir until creamy.

3 Arrange kofta kebabs on hot lightly greased barbecue grill or flatplate. Cook 10 minutes, turning frequently, until browned and cooked through. Serve with Tahini Dressing and grilled tomato halves, if desired.

COOK'S FILE

Storage time: Cook kebabs just before serving. Tahini Dressing can be made a day ahead.

LAMB CUTLETS WITH MINT GREMOLATA

Preparation time: 15 minutes
Cooking time: 10 minutes
Serves 4

4 tablespoons fresh mint leaves
1 tablespoon fresh flat-leaf parsley
2 cloves garlic
1½ tablespoons lemon rind (white pith removed), cut into thin strips
2 tablespoons extra virgin olive oil
8 French-trimmed lamb cutlets
2 carrots
2 zucchini
1 tablespoon lemon juice

1 To make the gremolata, finely chop the mint, parsley, garlic and lemon strips, then combine well.
2 Heat a barbecue plate or chargrill pan or to very hot. Lightly brush with 1 tablespoon of the oil. Cook the cutlets over medium heat for 2 minutes on each side, or until cooked to your liking. Remove the cutlets and cover to keep warm.
3 Trim the ends from the carrots and zucchini and, using a sharp vegetable peeler, peel the vegetables lengthways into ribbons. Heat the remaining oil in a large saucepan, add the vegetables and toss over medium heat for 3–5 minutes, or until sautéed but tender.
4 Divide the cutlets among the serving plates, sprinkle the cutlets with the gremolata and drizzle with the lemon juice. Serve with the vegetable ribbons.

COOK'S FILE
Hint: Use a vegetable peeler to remove the rind from the lemon.

LAMB SATAYS WITH CHILLI PEANUT SAUCE

Preparation time: 25 minutes
+ 1 hour marinating
Total cooking time: 15 minutes
Serves 4

600 g lamb fillets
2 cloves garlic, crushed
½ teaspoon ground black pepper
6 teaspoons finely chopped lemon
   grass
2 tablespoons soy sauce
2 teaspoons sugar
¼ teaspoon ground turmeric

CHILLI PEANUT SAUCE

1½ cups unsalted roasted peanuts
2 tablespoons vegetable oil
1 medium onion, roughly chopped
1 clove garlic, roughly chopped
1 tablespoon sambal oelek
1 tablespoon soft brown sugar
1 tablespoon kecap manis (sweet soy
   sauce) or soy sauce
1 teaspoon grated ginger
1½ teaspoons ground coriander
1 cup coconut cream
¼ teaspoon ground turmeric
salt and pepper, to taste

1 Trim lamb of excess fat and sinew. Then cut the lamb into thin strips, thread onto skewers, bunching strips along three-quarters of the length. Place satays in shallow non-metal dish. Combine garlic, pepper, lemon grass, soy sauce, sugar and turmeric in a small bowl; mix well. Brush marinade over skewered meat, set aside for 1 hour. Prepare and heat the barbecue.
2 To make Chilli Peanut Sauce, process peanuts in food processor bowl 10 seconds or until coarsely ground. Heat oil in small pan. Add onion and garlic, cook over medium heat 3–4 minutes or until translucent. Add sambal oelek, sugar, kecap manis, ginger and coriander. Cook, stirring 2 minutes. Add coconut cream, turmeric and processed peanuts. Reduce heat, cook 3 minutes or until thickened; season with salt and pepper. Remove from heat.
3 Place mixture in food processor bowl. Process 20 seconds or until almost smooth. Spoon into individual serving dishes to cool. Barbecue satays on hot lightly greased grill or flatplate 2–3 minutes each side or until browned.

COOK'S FILE

Storage time: Barbecue the satays just before serving. The satays can be marinated up to 2 days in advance. Store, covered, in refrigerator. Sauce can be made 3–4 days in advance. Store in a screwtop jar in refrigerator.
Variation: Salted roasted peanuts can be used to make the Chilli Peanut Sauce. (Taste the sauce before adding any additional salt.)
Hint: Chilli Peanut Sauce can be used over any beef or vegetable satays.

1

2

3

BARBECUED PORK SPARE RIBS

Preparation time: 15 minutes
+ 3 hours marinating
Total cooking time: 30 minutes
Serves 4–6

1 kg American-style pork spare ribs
2 cups tomato sauce
1/2 cup sherry
2 tablespoons soy sauce
2 tablespoons honey
3 cloves garlic, crushed
1 tablespoon grated fresh
   ginger

1 Trim the spare ribs of excess fat and sinew. Then cut racks of ribs into pieces, so that each piece has three or four ribs. Combine tomato sauce, sherry, soy sauce, honey, garlic and ginger in a large pan; mix well.
2 Add ribs to mixture. Bring to the boil. Reduce heat and simmer, covered, 15 minutes. Move ribs occasionally to ensure even cooking. Transfer ribs and sauce to shallow non-metal dish; allow to cool. Refrigerate, covered with plastic wrap, several hours or overnight. Prepare and heat barbecue 1 hour before cooking.
3 Place the ribs on hot lightly oiled barbecue grill or flatplate. Cook over the hottest part of the fire for 15 minutes, turning and brushing with sauce occasionally. Serve with barbecued corn on the cob and potato salad, if desired.

COOK'S FILE

Storage time: Ribs can be prepared up to 2 days in advance. Store the ribs, covered, in the refrigerator. Barbecue just before serving.
Note: American-style pork spare ribs come in rack form. They can be eaten easily with the fingers if they are separated into individual ribs. Serve ribs with other pre-dinner finger foods next to a dipping sauce, such as barbecue or tomato, and a generous supply of napkins.

PORK LOIN CHOPS WITH APPLE CHUTNEY

Preparation time: 20 minutes
+ 3 hours marinating
Total cooking time: 25 minutes
Serves 6

6 pork loin chops
1/3 cup white wine
2 tablespoons oil
2 tablespoons honey
1 1/2 teaspoons ground cumin
2 cloves garlic, crushed

APPLE CHUTNEY
3 medium green apples
1/2 cup apple juice
1/2 cup fruit chutney
15 g butter

1 Trim pork chops of excess fat and sinew. Combine wine, oil, honey, cumin and garlic in small jug; mix well. Place chops in shallow non-metal dish; pour marinade over. Store, covered with plastic wrap, in refrigerator several hours or overnight, turning occasionally. Prepare and heat barbecue 1 hour before cooking.
2 Place chops on hot lightly oiled barbecue grill or flatplate. Cook for 8 minutes each side or until tender, turning once. Serve immediately with Apple Chutney.

3 To make Apple Chutney, peel apples and cut into small cubes. Place in small pan; cover with apple juice. Bring to the boil, reduce heat and simmer, covered, 7 minutes or until completely soft. Add chutney and butter; stir to combine. Serve the chutney warm.

COOK'S FILE
Storage time: Chops can be marinated up to 1 day in advance. Barbecue just before serving. Apple Chutney can be made 1 day in advance. Store, covered, in refrigerator and reheat gently to serve.
Hint: Apple Chutney can be used on roast pork, lamb chops, chicken cutlets or as a relish with a cheese plate. Serve warm or cold.

GINGER-ORANGE PORK STEAKS

Preparation time: 15 minutes
+ 3 hours marinating
Total cooking time: 20 minutes
Serves 6

6 pork butterfly steaks (200 g each)
1 cup ginger wine
1/2 cup orange marmalade
2 tablespoons oil
1 tablespoon grated ginger

1 Trim the pork steaks of excess fat and sinew. Combine wine, marmalade, oil and ginger in small jug; mix well. Place steaks in shallow non-metal dish; pour marinade over. Store, covered with plastic wrap, in refrigerator several hours or overnight, turning occasionally. Prepare and heat barbecue 1 hour before cooking. Drain pork steaks; reserve marinade.
2 Place pork on hot lightly oiled barbecue grill or flatplate. Cook 5 minutes each side or until tender, turning once.

3 While meat is cooking, place reserved marinade in small pan. Bring to the boil; reduce heat and simmer 5 minutes until marinade has reduced and thickened slightly. Pour over pork steaks immediately.

COOK'S FILE
Storage time: This recipe best barbecued close to serving.
Hint: Steaks of uneven thickness may curl during cooking. To prevent this, leave a layer of fat on the outside of the steak and make a few, deep cuts in the fat prior to cooking. Remove fat before serving.

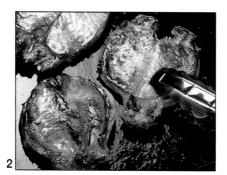

Pork Loin Chops with Apple Chutney (top)
Ginger-Orange Pork Steaks.

SWEET AND SOUR MARINATED PORK KEBABS

Preparation time: 30 minutes
+ 3 hours marinating
Total cooking time: 20 minutes
Serves 6

1 kg pork fillets
1 large red capsicum
1 large green capsicum
425 g can pineapple pieces
1 cup orange juice
¼ cup white vinegar
2 tablespoons soft brown sugar

2 teaspoons chilli garlic sauce
2 teaspoons cornflour

1 To make Sweet and Sour Sauce, place remaining marinade in small pan. Mix cornflour with a tablespoon of the marinade in small bowl until smooth; add to pan. Stir over medium heat until mixture boils and thickens; transfer to small serving bowl. Cover surface with plastic wrap; leave to cool.
2 Trim pork of excess fat and sinew. Cut meat into 2.5 cm cubes. Cut each capsicum into 2 cm squares. Drain the pineapple and reserve juice. Thread the meat, alternately with the capsicum and pineapple, onto skewers. Combine reserved pineapple

juice with orange juice, vinegar, sugar and sauce. Place kebabs in a shallow non-metal dish, pour half the juice mixture over. Cover and refrigerate for several hours or overnight, turning occasionally. Prepare and heat the barbecue 1 hour before cooking.
3 Place meat on a hot lightly oiled barbecue or flatplate and cook for 15 minutes, turning occasionally, until tender. Serve kebabs with Sweet and Sour Sauce.

COOK'S FILE

Storage time: Kebabs can be marinated up to 1 day in advance.

1

3

THAI-SPICED PORK TENDERLOIN AND GREEN MANGO SALAD

Preparation time: 45 minutes
+ 2 hours refrigeration
Total cooking time: 10 minutes
Serves 4 as a main
(6 as an entrée)

2 stems lemon grass (white part only),
    thinly sliced
1 clove garlic
2 red Asian shallots
1 tablespoon coarsely chopped fresh
    ginger
1 red bird's-eye chilli, seeded
1 tablespoon fish sauce
½ cup (15 g) fresh coriander leaves
1 teaspoon grated lime rind
1 tablespoon lime juice
2 tablespoons oil
2 pork tenderloins, trimmed
steamed jasmine rice (optional)

DRESSING

1 large red chilli, seeded and finely
    chopped
2 cloves garlic, finely chopped
3 fresh coriander roots, finely
    chopped
1¼ tablespoons grated palm sugar
2 tablespoons fish sauce
¼ cup (60 ml) lime juice

SALAD

2 green mangoes or 1 small green
    papaya, peeled, pitted and cut into
    julienne strips
1 carrot, grated
½ cup (45 g) bean sprouts
½ red onion, thinly sliced
3 tablespoons roughly chopped fresh
    mint
3 tablespoons roughly chopped fresh
    coriander leaves
3 tablespoons roughly chopped fresh
    Vietnamese mint

1 Place the lemon grass, garlic, shallots, ginger, chilli, fish sauce, coriander, lime rind, lime juice and oil in a blender or food processor and process until a coarse paste forms. Transfer to a non-metallic dish. Coat the pork in the marinade, cover and refrigerate for at least 2 hours, but no longer than 4 hours.

2 To make the Salad Dressing, mix all the ingredients together in a large bowl.
3 Combine all the salad ingredients in a large bowl.
4 Heat the barbecue or a chargrill pan and cook the pork over medium heat for 4–5 minutes each side, or until cooked through. Remove from

the heat, rest for 5 minutes, then slice.
5 Toss the dressing and salad together. Season to taste with salt and cracked black pepper. Arrange the sliced pork in a circle in the centre of each plate and top with salad. To make this into a main course, serve the pork with steamed jasmine rice, if desired.

Process the marinade ingredients to a coarse paste.

Cook the pork on a chargrill pan until cooked through.

MARINADES AND SAUCES FOR MEAT

Enhance the flavour of beef, lamb or pork by soaking or basting them in these tasty marinades. Sauces are the perfect partner to barbecued meat.

LEMON AND WINE MARINADE

Combine 2 tablespoons lemon juice, 2 teaspoons grated lemon rind, 1 clove crushed garlic, ¼ cup white wine, ¼ cup olive oil, 2 tablespoons soft brown sugar, 1 tablespoon each of chopped rosemary and lemon thyme. Mix well. Marinate lamb or chicken several hours or overnight in refrigerator. Turn meat occasionally; keep covered.

TERIYAKI MARINADE

Combine ¼ cup soy sauce, 2 tablespoons teriyaki sauce, 3 teaspoons grated fresh ginger, 1–2 cloves crushed garlic, 2 tablespoons soft brown sugar, ¼ cup chicken or beef stock and 2–3 tablespoons sweet sherry. Mix well. Marinate beef, pork or chicken several hours or overnight in refrigerator. Turn meat occasionally; keep covered.

SPICED YOGHURT MARINADE

Combine 1 cup plain yoghurt, 1 finely chopped onion, ¾ teaspoon each of ground coriander, cumin, garam masala and cinnamon, 1 clove crushed garlic, ½ teaspoon ground ginger, 1 teaspoon sugar, salt, pepper and pinch of cardamom. Mix well. Marinate lamb or beef several hours or overnight in refrigerator. Turn meat occasionally; keep covered.

APRICOT AND ONION MARINADE

Combine ⅓ cup apricot nectar, 1 teaspoon Worcestershire sauce, 1 tablespoon each of oil and malt vinegar, 1–2 tablespoons French onion soup mix and 2–3 finely sliced spring onions. Mix well. Marinate pork or chicken several hours or overnight in refrigerator. Turn meat occasionally; keep covered. (Add ¼ cup red or white wine to this marinade, if desired.)

MUSTARD AND HERB MARINADE

Combine ¼ cup olive oil, 2 tablespoons balsamic vinegar, 2 teaspoons soft brown sugar,

2–3 teaspoons Dijon, German or wholegrain mustard, 1–2 teaspoons mixed dried herbs, 1 tablespoon chopped fresh parsley, salt and pepper. Mix well. Marinate beef or lamb several hours or overnight in refrigerator. Turn meat occasionally; keep covered.

TOMATO SAUCE

Heat 1 tablespoon olive oil and 20 g butter in small pan. Add 1 small finely chopped onion, 1 clove crushed garlic and 1–2 teaspoons Italian dried mixed herbs. Cook 2–3 minutes or until onion is soft. Stir in 2 large chopped ripe tomatoes, ½ cup tomato purée and 2 teaspoons balsamic vinegar. Cook 3–4 minutes.

Remove from heat. Process until smooth. Season with salt and pepper. Serve warm or cold with burgers, sausages, steak or fish.

GARLIC HERB HOLLANDAISE

Place 2 egg yolks in food processor bowl or blender. With motor constantly running, add 160 g melted butter in thin stream. Process until thick and creamy. Add 2–3 table-spoons lemon juice or white wine vinegar, 1 tablespoon each of chopped chives, basil, oregano and 1 clove crushed garlic. Season with salt and pepper. Process 10 seconds to combine. Serve with fish, seafood, chicken or beef.

CORIANDER MAYONNAISE

Place 3 egg yolks in food processor or blender. With motor constantly running, add ¾ cup light olive oil in thin stream. Process until thick and creamy. Add 2 tablespoons lemon juice and 1–2 tablespoons chopped coriander. Process until combined. Season with salt and pepper. Add crushed garlic clove, or vary the taste with your own herb selection. Serve with chicken, fish or veal.

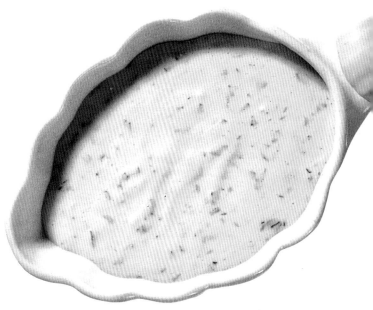

CHICKEN

HONEY GLAZED CHICKEN BREASTS

Preparation time: 6 minutes
+ 20 minutes marinating
Total cooking time: 10 minutes
Serves 6

6 chicken breast fillets (1 kg)
50 g butter, softened
$\frac{1}{4}$ cup honey
$\frac{1}{4}$ cup barbecue sauce
2 teaspoons seeded mustard

1 Trim chicken of excess fat and sinew. Remove skin. Use a sharp knife to make three or four diagonal slashes across one side of each chicken breast. Prepare and heat barbecue.

2 Combine butter, honey, barbecue sauce and mustard in a small bowl. Spread half of the marinade thickly over the slashed side of the chicken; cover. Set remaining marinade aside. Stand chicken at room temperature for 20 minutes.

3 Place chicken breasts, slashed-side up, on hot, lightly greased barbecue grill or flatplate. Cook 2–3 minutes each side or until tender. Brush with reserved marinade several times during cooking. Serve hot with buttered ribbon noodles, if desired.

COOK'S FILE
Storage time: Barbecue chicken just before serving. Chicken can be marinated overnight, provided it is kept, covered, in the refrigerator. The longer the chicken is marinated, the more it will take on flavour, so if chicken is not desired overly sweet, marinate for a short time only.
Hints: Crisply fried onion is an great accompaniment to this dish. Peel 4 medium onions, cut in half and slice finely. Heat 4 cups of good quality vegetable oil or olive oil to medium-hot. Place onion in a frying basket, lower into the oil. (If oil begins to foam, lift basket out, set aside 30 seconds, then try again.) Cook 10–15 minutes or until onion is well browned and crisp. Drain on paper towels. Serve the chicken immediately.
Leftover cooked chicken can be shredded and served mixed through a green salad or sliced thickly and made up into sandwiches for a picnic.
Notes: When honey is cooked, its sugars caramelise and some of its flavour is lost. For a distinctive taste to this dish, use honeys with a strong, dark flavour, such as leatherwood, lavender or rosemary. Lighter honeys, such as yellow box, orange blossom or clover, will sweeten and glaze the meat without necessarily affecting its flavour. Usually the paler the honey, the milder its flavour.

2

3

THAI DRUMSTICKS

Preparation time: 10 minutes
+ 2 hours marinating
Total cooking time: 1 hour
Serves 6

3 tablespoons red curry paste
1 cup (250 ml) coconut milk
2 tablespoons lime juice
4 tablespoons finely chopped fresh
    coriander leaves
12 chicken drumsticks, scored
2 bunches (1 kg) baby bok choy
2 tablespoons soy sauce
1 tablespoon oil

1 Combine the curry paste, coconut milk, lime juice and coriander in a bowl. Place the chicken in a flat dish and pour on the marinade. Cover and marinate in the refrigerator for 2 hours, or overnight if time permits.
2 Cook the chicken on a barbecue or chargrill plate for 50–60 minutes, or until cooked through.
3 Trim the bok choy and combine with the soy sauce and oil, then cook on the barbecue or in a wok for 3–4 minutes, or until just wilted. Serve the chicken on a bed of bok choy.

CHICKEN FAJITAS

Preparation time: 35 minutes
+ 3 hours marinating
Total cooking time: 10 minutes
Serves 4

4 chicken breast fillets
2 tablespoons olive oil
¼ cup lime juice
2 cloves garlic, crushed
1 teaspoon ground cumin
¼ cup chopped fresh coriander leaves
8 flour tortillas
1 tablespoon olive oil, extra
2 medium onions, sliced

2 medium green capsicum, cut into thin strips
1 cup grated cheddar cheese
1 large avocado, sliced
1 cup bottled tomato salsa

1 Trim chicken of fat and sinew. Cut chicken into thin strips. Place in shallow non-metal dish. Combine oil, juice, garlic, coriander and cumin in jug; mix well. Pour over chicken. Store, covered, in the refrigerator for several hours or overnight. Heat barbecue 1 hour before cooking.
2 Wrap tortillas in foil and place on a cool part of the barbecue grill for 10 minutes to warm. Heat oil on flat-plate. Cook onion and capsicum for

5 minutes or until soft. Push over to a cooler part of the plate to keep warm.
3 Place chicken and marinade on flatplate and cook 5 minutes until just tender. Transfer chicken, vegetables and wrapped tortillas to serving platter. Make up individual fajitas by placing chicken, cooked onion and capsicum, grated cheese and avocado over flat tortillas. Top with salsa. Roll up to enclose filling.

COOK'S FILE

Storage time: Chicken can be marinated up to 2 days in advance.

1

2

3

PIRRI-PIRRI CHICKEN

Preparation time: 5 minutes
+ 1 hour marinating
Total cooking time: 1 hour
Serves 4

6 birdseye chillies, finely chopped,
with seeds
1 teaspoon coarse salt
½ cup (125 ml) olive oil
¾ cup (185 ml) cider vinegar
1 clove garlic, crushed
4 chicken Maryland pieces
4 lemon wedges

1 Combine the chilli, salt, olive oil,
vinegar and garlic in a jar. Seal the
jar and shake well to combine the
ingredients.

2 Place the chicken pieces in a
shallow dish and pour on the
marinade. Cover and marinate for
1 hour, or overnight if time permits.
3 Cook the chicken on a hot
barbecue or chargrill plate, or under
a hot grill, as close to the flame as
possible, basting regularly with the
marinade, for 50–60 minutes, or
until the chicken is cooked through
and the skin begins to crisp. Serve
with lemon wedges, corn cobs and
steamed green beans.

COOK'S FILE

Note: Any chicken cut that is still on the
bone can be used in this recipe. Pirri-
pirri is also excellent for barbecuing
prawns. Remove the seeds from the
chillies to make a milder tasting dish.

ASIAN BARBECUED CHICKEN

Preparation time: 10 minutes
+ 2 hours marinating
Total cooking time: 25 minutes
Serves 4–6

2 cloves garlic, finely chopped
¼ cup (60 ml) hoisin sauce
3 teaspoons light soy sauce
3 teaspoons honey
2 tablespoons tomato sauce
    or sweet chilli sauce
1 teaspoon sesame oil
2 spring onions, finely sliced
1.5 kg chicken wings

1 To make the marinade, combine the garlic, hoisin sauce, soy, honey, tomato sauce, sesame oil and spring onion in a small bowl.

2 Pour over the chicken wings, cover and marinate in the refrigerator for 2 hours, or overnight if time permits.

3 Place the chicken on a barbecue or chargrill and cook, in batches, turning once, for 20–25 minutes, or until cooked and golden brown. Baste with the marinade during cooking. Heat any remaining marinade in a pan until boiling and serve as a sauce. Serve with a green salad.

COOK'S FILE

Note: The chicken can also be baked in a moderate 180°C (350°F/Gas 4) oven for 30 minutes, and turned halfway through cooking.

Variation: Other cuts of chicken, such as drumsticks or breast or thigh fillets could be substituted, if desired.

1

2

3

LIME AND CORIANDER CHARGRILLED CHICKEN

Preparation time: 15 minutes
+ 1 hour marinating
Cooking time: 15 minutes
Serves 4

3 teaspoons finely grated fresh ginger
½ cup (25 g) chopped fresh coriander
 leaves
1½ teaspoons grated lime rind
⅓ cup (80 ml) lime juice
4 skinless chicken breast fillets
 (about 750 g), trimmed
1¼ cups (250 g) jasmine rice
2 tablespoons oil
3 zucchini, cut into wedges
4 large flat mushrooms, stalks
 trimmed

1 Combine the ginger, coriander, lime rind and 2 tablespoons of the lime juice. Spread 2 teaspoons of the herb mixture over each fillet and season well. Marinate for 1 hour. Combine the remaining herb mixture with the remaining lime juice in a screwtop jar. Set aside until needed.
2 Bring a large saucepan of water to the boil. Add the rice and cook for 12 minutes, stirring occasionally. Drain well.
3 Meanwhile, heat a barbecue plate or chargrill pan to medium and lightly brush with oil. Brush the zucchini and mushrooms with the remaining oil. Place the chicken on the barbecue plate and cook on each side for 4–5 minutes, or until cooked through. Add the vegetables during the last 5 minutes of cooking, and turn them frequently until browned on the outside and just softened.

Cover with foil until ready to serve.
4 Divide the rice among four serving bowls. Cut the chicken fillets into long thick strips, then arrange on top of the rice. Shake the dressing well and drizzle over the chicken and serve with the chargrilled vegetables.

COOK'S FILE
Note: Allow 5 minutes for the chargrill pan to heat evenly to medium heat. Do not cook on a smoking hot grill or the chicken will singe, overcooking the outside and not evenly throughout.

MISO YAKITORI CHICKEN

Preparation time: 30 minutes
Total cooking time: 20 minutes
Serves 4

3 tablespoons yellow or red miso
    paste
2 tablespoons sugar
¼ cup (60 ml) sake
2 tablespoons mirin
1 kg chicken thighs, boned (skin on)
1 cucumber
2 spring onions, cut into 2 cm pieces

1 Soak 12 long wooden bamboo skewers in cold water for at least 10 minutes. Place the miso, sugar, sake and mirin in a small saucepan over medium heat and cook, stirring well, for 2 minutes, or until the sauce is smooth and the sugar has dissolved completely.

2 Cut the chicken into 2.5 cm cubes. Seed the cucumber and cut into 2 cm batons. Thread the chicken, cucumber and spring onion alternately onto the skewers—you should have 3 pieces of chicken, 3 pieces of cucumber and 3 pieces of spring onion per skewer.

3 Heat the barbecue or a grill plate and cook over high heat, turning occasionally, for 10 minutes, or until the chicken is almost cooked. Brush with the miso sauce and continue cooking, then turn and brush the other side. Repeat this process once or twice until the chicken and vegetables are cooked. Serve immediately with steamed rice and salad.

Remove the bones from the chicken thighs with a sharp knife.

Remove the seeds from the centre of the cucumber, then cut into batons.

Brush the chicken and vegetables with the miso sauce during cooking.

CHARGRILLED CHICKEN SALAD WITH ROCKET AND CANNELLINI BEANS

Preparation time: 10 minutes
Total cooking time: 20 minutes
Serves 4

⅓ cup (80 ml) lemon juice
3 cloves garlic, crushed
¼ cup (15 g) chopped fresh basil
1 teaspoon soft brown sugar
½ cup (125 ml) olive oil
4 chicken breast fillets
400 g can cannellini beans, rinsed
    and drained
100 g small rocket leaves

1 Prepare the vinaigrette by whisking together the lemon juice, garlic, basil, sugar and olive oil. Season.

2 Pour a third of the dressing over the chicken breasts to coat. Heat the barbecue and chargrill the chicken, in batches, for 10 minutes, turning once, or until cooked through.

3 Meanwhile, combine the beans and rocket with the remaining vinaigrette, toss well and season. Slice the chicken across the grain into 1.5 cm pieces. Serve the rocket and beans topped with the sliced chicken.

1

2

3

CHICKEN TIKKA KEBABS

Preparation time: 10 minutes
+ 30 minutes soaking
+ 2 hours marinating
Total cooking time: 10 minutes
Serves 4

10 chicken thigh fillets, cubed
1 red onion, cut into wedges
¼ cup (60 ml) tikka paste
½ cup (125 ml) coconut milk
2 tablespoons lemon juice

1 Soak 8 skewers in water for 30 minutes to prevent burning. Thread 2 pieces of chicken and a wedge of onion alternately along each skewer.

2 Combine the tikka paste, coconut milk and lemon juice in a jar with a lid. Season and shake well to combine. Pour the mixture over the skewers and marinate for 2 hours, or overnight if time permits.

3 Heat a barbecue or grill plate and cook the skewers, basting, for 7–8 minutes, or until the chicken is cooked through. Serve with boiled brown rice and a crisp green salad.

COOK'S FILE

Note: Any leftover marinade can be heated to boiling and used as a sauce.

PERSIAN CHICKEN SKEWERS

Preparation time: 10 minutes
+ 30 minutes soaking
+ overnight marinating
Total cooking time: 10 minutes
Serves 4

2 teaspoons ground cardamom
¼ teaspoon ground turmeric
1 teaspoon ground allspice
4 cloves garlic, crushed
¼ cup (60 ml) lemon juice
3 tablespoons olive oil
4 large chicken thigh fillets,
    excess fat removed

1 Soak 8 wooden skewers in water for 30 minutes to prevent them burning. To make the marinade, whisk together the spices, garlic, lemon juice and oil. Season with salt and freshly ground black pepper.
2 Cut each thigh fillet into 3–4 cm cubes. Toss the cubes in the spice mixture. Thread the chicken onto skewers and place on a tray. Cover and refrigerate overnight.
3 Heat a barbecue plate or grill and cook the skewers for 4 minutes each side, or until cooked through. Serve with a green salad, lemon wedges and plain yoghurt, if desired.

TERIYAKI CHICKEN WINGS

Preparation time: 15 minutes
+ 3 hours marinating
Total cooking time: 13 minutes
Serves 4

8 chicken wings
¼ cup soy sauce
2 tablespoons sherry
2 teaspoons grated ginger
1 clove garlic, crushed
1 tablespoon honey

1 Wash chicken wings and pat dry with paper towel. Trim any excess fat from wings, and tuck tips under to form a triangle.

2 Place wings in shallow non-metal dish. Combine soy sauce, sherry, ginger, garlic and honey in a jug; mix well. Pour over chicken. Store, covered with plastic wrap, in refrigerator several hours or overnight. Prepare and light barbecue 1 hour before cooking. Lightly brush two sheets of aluminium foil with oil. Place 4 wings in a single layer on each piece of foil; wrap completely.

3 Place parcels on hot barbecue grill or flatplate 10 minutes. Remove parcels from heat; unwrap. Place wings directly on lightly greased grill 3 minutes or until brown. Turn wings frequently and brush with any remaining marinade.

COOK'S FILE

Storage time: Chicken can be marinated up to 2 days in advance. Cook just before serving.

Variation: Marinade can also be used on beef or pork.

Note: Teriyaki marinade is available in the Asian section of most supermarkets.

CITRUS CHICKEN DRUMSTICKS

Preparation time: 20 minutes
+ 3 hours marinating
Total cooking time: 20 minutes
Serves 4

8 chicken drumsticks
⅓ cup orange juice
⅓ cup lemon juice

1 teaspoon grated orange rind
1 teaspoon grated lemon rind
1 teaspoon sesame oil
1 tablespoon olive oil
1 spring onion, finely chopped

1 Wash drumsticks and pat dry. Trim any excess fat and score thickest part of chicken with a knife. Place in a shallow non-metal dish.
2 Combine juices, rinds, oils and spring onion in jug, pour over chicken. Store, covered with plastic wrap, in refrigerator several hours or overnight, turning occasionally. Drain chicken, reserve marinade. Prepare and heat barbecue 1 hour before cooking.
3 Cook drumsticks on hot lightly oiled barbecue grill or flatplate 15–20 minutes or until tender. Brush occasionally with the reserved marinade. Serve immediately.

COOK'S FILE
Storage time: This dish is best cooked just before serving.

1

2

3

TANDOORI WEBER CHICKEN

Preparation time: 15 minutes
+ 4 hours marinating
Total cooking time: 1 hour
Serves 4

4 chicken Marylands (drumstick and thigh), skin removed
1 teaspoon salt
2 cloves garlic, crushed
1 tablespoon lemon juice
1 cup plain yoghurt
1½ teaspoons garam masala
½ teaspoon ground black pepper
½ teaspoon ground turmeric
2–3 drops red food colouring
olive oil, for basting

20–30 mesquite or hickory chips, for smoking

1 Place Marylands in a non-metal dish; rub with salt and garlic. Now combine lemon juice, yoghurt, garam masala, pepper and turmeric in a jug. Add food colouring to make the marinade an orange-red colour. Pour over the chicken, and coat evenly with the back of a spoon. Cover, set aside 4 hours, turning chicken every hour to redistributing the marinade. In the last hour of marinating, heat and prepare weber (kettle) barbecue for indirect cooking (see page 9).
2 When barbecue coals are covered with fine white ash, add mesquite or hickory chips to coals. Cover the barbecue and leave until the smoke is well established (about 5 minutes).

3 Brush barbecue grill with oil. Arrange Marylands on grill; put lid on barbecue. Smoke-cook for 45 minutes–1 hour or until chicken is well crisped. Brush chicken with oil several times during cooking. Serve with side salad and onion rings, if desired.

COOK'S FILE
Storage time: Cook the chicken just before serving.
Note: Tandoori chicken requires a slow heat. Do not place chicken on barbecue while the fire is still very hot. Test the heat of the fire before adding the chips. Hold your hand over the top grill. If you can leave your hand, comfortably, for 4–5 seconds the fire is low enough to use. If fire is too hot, allow to burn down 15–30 minutes more.

1

2

3

*Citrus Chicken Drumsticks (top)
and Tandoori Weber Chicken.*

BUFFALO CHICKEN WINGS WITH RANCH DRESSING

Preparation time: 25 minutes
+ 3 hours marinating
Total cooking time: 10 minutes
Serves 4

8 large chicken wings (900 g)
2 teaspoons black pepper
2 teaspoons garlic salt
2 teaspoons onion powder
olive oil, for deep frying
½ cup tomato sauce
2 tablespoons Worcestershire sauce
20 g butter, melted
2 teaspoons sugar
Tabasco sauce, to taste

RANCH DRESSING
½ cup whole egg mayonnaise
½ cup sour cream
2 tablespoons lemon juice
2 tablespoons chopped chives
salt and white pepper to taste

1 Wash wings thoroughly and pat dry with paper towels. Cut tips off each wing; discard. Bend each wing back to snap joint and cut through to create two pieces. Combine pepper, garlic salt and onion powder. Using fingers, rub mixture into each piece.
2 Heat oil to moderately hot in deep heavy-based pan. Cook chicken pieces in batches 2 minutes; remove with tongs or slotted spoon and drain on paper towels.
3 Transfer chicken to non-metal bowl or shallow dish. Combine sauces, butter, sugar and Tabasco and pour over chicken; stir to coat. Refrigerate, covered, several hours or overnight. Prepare and heat barbecue 1 hour before cooking.
4 Place chicken on hot lightly oiled barbecue grill or flatplate. Cook 5 minutes, turning and brushing with marinade. Serve with Ranch Dressing. To make Ranch Dressing, combine mayonnaise, cream, juice, chives, salt and pepper in bowl, mix well.

COOK'S FILE
Storage time: Wings can be prepared up to 2 days in advance.

1

2

3

4

TANDOORI CHICKEN WITH YOGHURT DRESSING

Preparation time: 10 minutes
+ 1 hour marinating
Total cooking time: 30 minutes
Serves 4

½ cup (125 g) Greek-style plain yoghurt
2 tablespoons tandoori paste
2 cloves garlic, crushed
2 tablespoons lime juice
1½ teaspoons garam masala
2 tablespoons finely chopped fresh
    coriander leaves
6 chicken thigh fillets, excess fat
    removed

1   Combine the yoghurt, tandoori paste, garlic, lime juice, garam masala and coriander in a bowl and mix well.
2   Add the chicken, coat well, cover and refrigerate for at least 1 hour, or overnight if time permits.
3   Preheat a barbecue or chargrill plate and lightly brush with oil. Cook the chicken, in batches if necessary, for 10–15 minutes on medium heat, turning the chicken once and basting with the remaining marinade, until golden and cooked through. Serve with cucumber raita and naan bread.

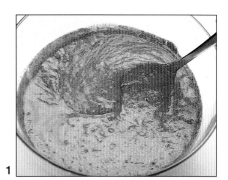

1

2

3

MIDDLE EASTERN BAKED CHICKEN

Preparation time: 30 minutes
Total cooking time: 1 hour
15 minutes
Serves 6

1.6 kg chicken
½ cup boiling water
½ cup instant couscous
4 pitted dates, chopped
4 dried apricots, chopped
1 tablespoon lime juice
1 tablespoon olive oil
20 g butter
1 medium onion, chopped
1–2 cloves garlic, chopped
1 teaspoon salt
¼ teaspoon cracked black
    pepper
1 teaspoon ground coriander
2 tablespoons chopped parsley
salt and pepper, extra
1 teaspoon ground cumin
1 tablespoon olive oil, extra

1 Prepare and heat the weber (kettle) barbecue for indirect cooking. (See page 9.) Place drip tray underneath top grill. Remove giblets and any large deposits of fat from chicken. Wipe and pat dry chicken with paper towel. Pour boiling water over couscous and set aside 15 minutes for couscous to swell and soften. Soak dates and apricots in lime juice; set aside.
2 Heat oil and butter in pan, add onion and garlic; cook 3–4 minutes until translucent. Remove from heat; add couscous and soaked dried fruit, salt, pepper, coriander and parsley. Mix well. Spoon stuffing into chicken cavity and close with toothpicks or a skewer. Tie legs together with string.
3 Rub chicken skin all over with combined salt, pepper, cumin and extra oil. Place chicken in the centre of a large piece of greased foil. Gather edges of foil and wrap securely.
4 Place the parcel on barbecue grill over drip tray. Cover barbecue, cook 50 minutes. Open the foil, crimping the edges to form a tray to retain most

of the cooking liquids. Cook a further 20 minutes or until chicken is tender and golden. Remove from heat and stand 5–6 minutes before carving.

COOK'S FILE

Storage: Bake chicken just before serving. Chicken can be stuffed 3–4 hours in advance.
Hint: Leftover chicken can be sliced and served with a salad of avocado, sliced onion and orange segments.

CHICKEN BREASTS WITH SALSA VERDE

Preparation time: 10 minutes
Total cooking time: 10 minutes
Serves 6

1 clove garlic
2 cups (60 g) firmly packed fresh
   flat-leaf parsley
1/3 cup (80 ml) extra virgin
   olive oil
3 tablespoons chopped fresh
   dill
1½ tablespoons Dijon mustard
1 tablespoon sherry vinegar
1 tablespoon baby capers, drained
6 large chicken breast fillets

1 Place all the ingredients, except the chicken, in a food processor or blender and process until almost smooth.
2 Lightly grease a barbecue or chargrill plate and heat to very hot. Cook the chicken fillets for 4–5 minutes each side, or until cooked through.
3 Cut each chicken fillet into 3 on the diagonal and arrange on six serving plates. Top with a spoonful of Salsa Verde and season to taste. Serve with salad or vegetables.

COOK'S FILE

Note: The Salsa Verde can be made a day ahead to save preparation time.

1

2

3

Thread one chicken strip onto each skewer; flatten it out on the skewer.

Add a little oil to the paste to assist the processing.

Peanut Sauce will thicken when it has been standing.

During cooking, sprinkle the chicken with oil and brown sugar.

CHICKEN SATAY WITH PEANUT SAUCE

Preparation time: 40 minutes
+ 30 minutes marinating
Total cooking time: 15–20 minutes
Serves 4

500 g (1 lb) chicken thigh fillets, trimmed
1 onion, roughly chopped
2 stems lemon grass (white part only), thinly sliced
4 cloves garlic
2 red chillies, chopped
2 teaspoons ground coriander
1 teaspoon ground cumin
1/2 teaspoon salt
1 tablespoon soy sauce
1/4 cup (60 ml/2 fl oz) oil
1 tablespoon soft brown sugar
cucumber slices and chopped roasted peanuts, to garnish

PEANUT SAUCE

1/2 cup (125 g/4 oz) crunchy peanut butter
1 cup (250 ml/8 fl oz) coconut milk
1/2 cup (125 ml/4 fl oz) water
1–2 tablespoons sweet chilli sauce
1 tablespoon soy sauce
2 teaspoons lemon juice

1 Soak 20 wooden skewers in cold water for 30 minutes. Cut the chicken into flattish thick strips about 6 cm (2½ inches) long and 2 cm (1 inch) wide. Thread 1 strip of chicken onto each skewer, flattening it on the skewer.

2 Process the onion, lemon grass, garlic, chillies, coriander, cumin, salt and soy sauce in a food processor, pulsing in short bursts, until smooth, adding a little oil to assist with the processing. Spread the mixture over the chicken, cover and refrigerate for 30 minutes.

3 To make the Peanut Sauce, stir all the ingredients in a heavy-based pan, over low heat, until the mixture boils. Remove from the heat. The sauce will thicken on standing.

4 Heat a chargrill or barbecue flatplate until very hot and brush with the remaining oil. Cook the chicken satays for 2–3 minutes on each side, sprinkling with a little oil and brown sugar. Serve the satays topped with Peanut Sauce and garnished with cucumber slices and peanuts.

INDONESIAN CHILLI CHICKEN

Preparation time: 15 minutes
+ 2 hours refrigeration
Total cooking time: 20 minutes
Serves 6

1 kg (2 lb) chicken thigh fillets
2 tablespoons lime juice
½ cup (125 ml/4 fl oz) sweet chilli sauce
3 tablespoons kecap manis

1 Trim any excess fat from the chicken thigh fillets and cut them in half. Transfer to a shallow non-metallic dish.
2 Place the lime juice, sweet chilli sauce and kecap manis in a bowl and whisk to combine.
3 Pour the marinade over the chicken, cover and refrigerate for 2 hours.
4 Chargrill on a barbecue or bake in a preheated moderately hot 200°C (400°F/Gas 6) oven for 20 minutes, or until the chicken is tender and cooked through and the marinade has caramelised.

COOK'S FILE
Note: Kecap manis (ketjap manis) is a thick Indonesian sauce, similar to—but sweeter than—soy sauce, and is generally flavoured with garlic and star anise. Store in a cool, dry place and refrigerate after opening. If not available, use soy sauce sweetened with a little soft brown sugar.

Trim the excess fat from the thigh fillets, and cut them in half.

For the marinade, whisk together the lime juice, chilli sauce and kecap manis.

Pour the marinade over the chicken, then cover and refrigerate.

BARBECUED GARLIC CHICKEN

Preparation time: 20 minutes
+ marinating
Total cooking time: 10 minutes
Serves 4

6 cloves garlic, crushed
1½ tablespoons cracked
    black peppercorns
½ cup chopped fresh coriander leaves
    and stems
4 coriander roots, chopped
⅓ cup lime juice
1 teaspoon soft brown sugar
1 teaspoon ground turmeric
2 teaspoons light soy sauce
4 chicken breast fillets

CUCUMBER AND TOMATO SALAD
1 small green cucumber, unpeeled
1 large egg tomato
¼ small red onion, sliced thinly
1 small red or green chilli,
    finely chopped
2 tablespoons fresh coriander leaves
2 tablespoons lime juice
1 teaspoon soft brown sugar
1 tablespoon fish sauce

1 Using a mortar and pestle or blender, blend the garlic, peppercorns, coriander, lime juice, sugar, turmeric and soy sauce until smooth. Transfer to a bowl.
2 Remove the tenderloins from underneath the fillets. Score the top surface of each fillet three times. Add the fillets and tenderloins to marinade; cover and refrigerate for 2 hours or overnight, turning occasionally.
3 To make Salad: Halve the cucumber and scoop out the seeds with a teaspoon. Cut into slices. Halve the tomato lengthways and slice.
4 Combine the cucumber, tomato, onion, chilli and coriander in a small bowl. Drizzle with the combined lime juice, sugar and fish sauce. Cook the chicken on a lightly greased barbecue hotplate for about 3 minutes on each side or until tender. The tenderloins will take less time to cook. Serve immediately with the salad.

Add the coriander root to the other ingredients and blend until smooth.

Separate the tenderloins from the chicken fillets by pulling them away.

Use a teaspoon to scoop the seeds out of the halved cucumber.

Drizzle the combined lime juice, sugar and fish sauce over the salad ingredients.

CAJUN CHICKEN WITH FRESH TOMATO AND CORN SALSA

Preparation time: 15 minutes
Cooking time: 15 minutes
Serves 4

2 corn cobs
2 vine-ripened tomatoes, diced
1 Lebanese cucumber, diced
2 tablespoons roughly chopped
   fresh coriander leaves
4 chicken breast fillets
   (about 200 g each)
¼ cup (35 g) Cajun seasoning
2 tablespoons lime juice
lime wedges, to serve

1 Cook the corn cobs in a saucepan of boiling water for 5 minutes, or until tender. Remove the kernels using a sharp knife and place in a bowl with the tomato, cucumber and coriander. Season to taste and mix well.

2 Heat a barbecue plate or chargrill pan to medium heat and brush lightly with oil. Pound each chicken breast between two sheets of plastic wrap with a mallet or rolling pin until 2 cm thick. Lightly coat the chicken with the Cajun seasoning and shake off any excess. Cook for 5 minutes on each side, or until just cooked through.

3 Just before serving, stir the lime juice into the salsa. Place a chicken breast on each serving plate and spoon the salsa on the side. Serve with the lime wedges, a green salad and crusty bread.

1

2

MARINADES AND GLAZES FOR CHICKEN

Give your barbecued chicken an international flavour with one of these delicious marinades. Chicken is best left to marinate overnight or for at least 2 hours before cooking.

LIME AND GINGER GLAZE

In a small pan combine ½ cup (160 g) lime marmalade, ¼ cup (60 ml) lime juice, 2 tablespoons sherry, 2 tablespoons soft brown sugar and 2 teaspoons finely grated ginger. Stir over low heat until it reaches a liquid consistency. Pour over 1 kg chicken wings and toss well to combine. Cover and refrigerate for 2 hours or overnight. Cook in a moderately hot 190°C (375°F/Gas 5) oven for 40 minutes, or until cooked through. Makes 1 cup (250 ml).

HONEY SOY MARINADE

Combine ¼ cup (90 g) honey, ¼ cup (60 ml) soy sauce, 1 crushed garlic clove, 2 tablespoons sake and ½ teaspoon Chinese five-spice powder. Remove excess fat from 500 g chicken thigh fillets. Pour on the marinade and toss well to combine. Cover and refrigerate for 2 hours or overnight. Cook on a hot barbecue for 10 minutes, turning once, or until cooked through. Makes ⅔ cup (170 ml).

REDCURRANT GLAZE

In a small saucepan combine 340 g jar redcurrant jelly, 2 tablespoons lemon juice, 2 tablespoons brandy and 1 teaspoon chopped fresh thyme, and stir over low heat until it reaches a liquid consistency. Pour the marinade over 500 g chicken breast fillets and toss well to combine. Cover and refrigerate for 2 hours or overnight. Cook in a moderately hot 190°C (375°F/Gas 5) oven for 20 minutes, or until cooked through. Makes 1 cup (250 ml).

Left, from top: Lime and ginger glaze, Honey soy marinade, Redcurrant glaze. Right, from top: Tandoori marinade; Mexican marinade; Thai marinade.

TANDOORI MARINADE

Soak 8 wooden skewers in water for 30 minutes to prevent burning. Combine 2 tablespoons tandoori paste, 1 cup (250 g) plain yoghurt and 1 tablespoon lime juice. Cut 500 g chicken tenderloins in half lengthways and thread onto skewers. Pour on the marinade and toss well to combine. Cover and refrigerate for 1–2 hours. Place under a hot grill and cook, basting with the marinade, until cooked through. Makes 1¼ cups (315 ml).

MEXICAN MARINADE

Combine 440 g bottled taco sauce, 2 tablespoons lime juice and 2 tablespoons chopped fresh coriander leaves. Pour the marinade over 1 kg scored chicken drumsticks and toss well to combine. Cover and refrigerate for 2 hours or overnight. Cook in a moderately hot 190°C (375°F/Gas 5) oven for 30 minutes, or until cooked through. Makes 1¼ cups (315 ml).

THAI MARINADE

Combine 2 tablespoons fish sauce, 2 tablespoons lime juice, 1 crushed garlic clove, 1 finely chopped stalk lemon grass, 2 teaspoons soft brown sugar, ½ cup (125 g) coconut cream and 2 tablespoons chopped fresh coriander leaves. Pour the marinade over 1 kg chicken drumsticks and toss well to combine. Cover and refrigerate for 2 hours or overnight. Cook in a moderately hot 190°C (375°F/Gas 5) oven for 30 minutes, or until cooked through. Makes ¾ cup (185 ml).

SEAFOOD

CHARGRILLED JUMBO PRAWNS

Preparation time: 15 minutes
+ 30 minutes marinating
Total cooking time: 5 minutes
Serves 4

8 (800 g) large raw king prawns
⅓ cup (80 ml) olive oil
3 cloves garlic, crushed
1 tablespoon sweet chilli sauce
2 tablespoons lime juice
¼ cup (60 ml) olive oil, extra
2 tablespoons lime juice, extra
mixed lettuce leaves, to serve

1 Remove the heads from the prawns. Using a sharp knife, cut through the centre of the prawns lengthways to form two halves, leaving tails and shells intact.
2 Place the olive oil, 2 crushed garlic cloves, sweet chilli sauce and lime juice in a large bowl, and mix together well. Add the prawns, toss to coat and marinate for 30 minutes. Meanwhile, combine the extra oil and lime juice and remaining garlic in a bowl. Heat a barbecue or chargrill plate until hot. Drain the prawns and cook cut-side-down first, brushing with the marinade, for 1–2 minutes each side, or until cooked. Divide the lettuce among four serving plates, place the prawns on top and spoon over the dressing. Season and serve immediately.

1.

2

VIETNAMESE FISH WITH ONIONS AND GINGER

Preparation time: 25 minutes
+ 20 minutes marinating
Total cooking time: 25 minutes
Serves 4–6

750g (1½ lb) small firm, white-fleshed fish, cleaned and scaled
2 teaspoons green peppercorns, finely crushed
2 teaspoons chopped red chillies
3 teaspoons fish sauce
2 teaspoons oil
1 tablespoon oil, extra

2 medium onions, finely sliced
4 cm (1½ inch) piece of fresh ginger, peeled and cut into very thin slices
3 cloves garlic, cut into very thin slivers
2 teaspoons sugar
4 spring onions, cut into 4 cm (1½ inch) pieces, then finely shredded

1 Wash the fish inside and out and pat dry with paper towels. Cut 2 diagonal slashes into the thickest part of the fish on both sides. In a food processor or mortar and pestle, grind the peppercorns, chillies and fish sauce to a paste and brush lightly over the fish. Allow to stand for 20 minutes.

2 Heat a barbecue or flatplate until very hot and lightly brush with oil. Cook the fish for 8 minutes on each side, or until the flesh flakes easily when tested. If grilling the fish, make sure it is not too close to the heat or it will burn.

3 While the fish is cooking, heat the extra oil in a pan and stir the onion over medium heat, until golden. Add the ginger, garlic and sugar; cook for 3 minutes. Place the fish on a serving plate, top with the onion mixture and sprinkle with spring onion. Serve immediately with wedges of lemon or lime.

Cut 2 diagonal slashes into the thickest part of the fish, using a sharp knife.

Lightly brush the chilli mixture over the surface of the fish.

Cook the finely sliced onion over medium heat, stirring until golden.

LEMON AND HERB TROUT

Preparation time: 20 minutes
Total cooking time: 15 minutes
Serves 4

¼ cup chopped fresh dill
2 tablespoons chopped fresh rosemary
⅓ cup coarsely chopped fresh
    flat-leaf parsley
2 teaspoons thyme leaves
6 teaspoons crushed green
    peppercorns
⅓ cup lemon juice
salt and pepper, to taste
2 lemons
4 whole fresh trout
⅓ cup dry white wine

HORSERADISH CREAM

1 tablespoon horseradish cream
½ cup sour cream
2 tablespoons cream
salt and pepper, to taste

LEMON SAUCE

2 egg yolks
150 g butter, melted
3–4 tablespoons lemon juice
salt and pepper, to taste

1 Prepare and heat barbecue. Lightly grease four large sheets of foil, each double-thickness. Combine herbs, peppercorns, juice, salt and pepper in bowl; mix well. Cut each lemon into eight slices, cut each slice in half. Place 2 lemon pieces in each fish cavity. Spoon the herb mixture into fish cavity.
2 Place each fish on foil layers, sprinkle each with 1 tablespoon of wine. Seal fish in foil to form neat parcels. Cook fish on barbecue for 10–15 minutes or until fish is just cooked through. (Test fish for doneness by gently flaking back flesh with a fork.) Stand fish, still wrapped in foil, 5 minutes, then serve with Horseradish Cream and Lemon Sauce.
3 To make Horseradish Cream, combine creams, salt and pepper in bowl; mix well. To make Lemon Sauce, place yolks in food processor. Process for 20 seconds or until blended. With motor constantly running, add the butter slowly in a thin, steady stream. Continue processing until all butter has been added and mixture is thick and creamy. Add juice and season with salt and pepper.

HONEYED PRAWN AND SCALLOP SKEWERS

Preparation time: 15 minutes
+ 3 hours marinating
Total cooking time: 5 minutes
Makes 8 skewers

500 g medium green prawns
250 g fresh scallops with corals intact
1/4 cup honey
2 tablespoons soy sauce
1/4 cup bottled barbecue sauce
2 tablespoons sweet sherry

1 Soak 8 wooden skewers in water. Remove heads from prawns. Peel and devein prawns, keeping tails intact. Clean scallops, removing brown vein.
2 Thread prawns and scallops alternately onto 8 skewers (about 3 of each per skewer). Place in base of shallow non-metal dish. Combine honey, sauces and sherry in jug and pour over skewers. Cover and refrigerate several hours or overnight.

Prepare and heat barbecue 1 hour before cooking.
3 Cook skewers on hot lightly greased barbecue flatplate 5 minutes or until cooked through. Brush frequently with marinade while cooking.

COOK'S FILE

Storage time: Store marinated skewers in refrigerator for up to 2 days. Cook just before serving.
Variation: Substitute cubes of firm-fleshed fish for prawns or scallops.

FISH PATTIES

Preparation time: 25 minutes
Total cooking time: 10 minutes
Makes 8–10 patties

750 g white fish fillets, cut into cubes
1 cup stale white breadcrumbs
3 spring onions, chopped
1/4 cup lemon juice
2 teaspoons seasoned pepper
1 tablespoon chopped fresh dill
2 tablespoons chopped fresh parsley
3/4 cup grated cheddar cheese
1 egg
1/2 cup plain flour, for dusting

HERBED MAYONNAISE
1/2 cup mayonnaise
1 tablespoon chopped
  fresh parsley
1 tablespoon chopped fresh chives
2 teaspoons chopped capers

1 Prepare and heat the barbecue. Place fish in food processor bowl. Process 20–30 seconds until smooth. Place minced fish in large bowl. Add breadcrumbs, spring onions, juice, pepper, herbs, cheese and egg. Mix well. Divide into 8–10 portions. Shape into round patties. Place on tray and refrigerate 15 minutes or until firm.
2 Toss patties in flour, shake off excess. Cook patties on hot lightly greased barbecue flatplate for 2–3 minutes each side until browned and cooked through. Serve with Herbed Mayonnaise and a green salad, if desired.
3 To make Herbed Mayonnaise, combine mayonnaise, herbs and capers in a small bowl; mix well.

COOK'S FILE

Storage time: This recipe is best made just before cooking. Patties should not be prepared more than a few hours in advance. After 2–3 hours the raw fish will begin to seep liquid which will cause the patties to fall apart during cooking.
Variation: Any firm-fleshed fish can be used in this recipe. Try whiting, perch, hake or cod.

Honeyed Prawn and Scallop Skewers (top)
Fish Patties.

THAI MARINATED FISH

Preparation time: 10 minutes
+ 3 hours marinating
Total cooking time: 15 minutes
Serves 4

1 medium-sized white-fleshed fish,
    cleaned and scaled
¾ cup fresh coriander leaves
2 cloves garlic, crushed
1 tablespoon soy sauce
1 tablespoon fish sauce

1 tablespoon sweet chilli sauce
2 teaspoons sesame oil
3 spring onions, finely chopped
2 teaspoons grated fresh ginger
1 tablespoon lime juice
1 teaspoon soft brown sugar

1 Place fish in large, shallow non-metal dish. Fill fish cavity with coriander leaves.
2 Combine the garlic, soy, fish and chilli sauces, oil, spring onions, ginger, juice and sugar in jug; mix well. Pour marinade over fish. Cover and refrig-erate several hours.

Prepare and heat the barbecue 1 hour before cooking.
3 Cook fish on hot, lightly greased flatplate for about 15 minutes, taking care not to burn skin. (Move fish away from the flame and dampen the fire if fish begins to stick to plate.) Brush fish frequently with marinade until flesh flakes back easily with a fork, and has turned opaque. Serve with egg noodles and citrus wedges.

COOK'S FILE
Storage time: Marinate fish for no more than 2–3 hours.

1   2   3

TUNA SKEWERS WITH MOROCCAN SPICES AND CHERMOULA

Preparation time: 20 minutes
+ 10 minutes marinating
Total cooking time: 5 minutes
Serves 4

800 g tuna steaks, cut into
3 cm cubes
2 tablespoons olive oil
½ teaspoon ground cumin
2 teaspoons grated lemon rind

CHERMOULA
3 teaspoons ground cumin
½ teaspoon ground coriander
2 teaspoons paprika
pinch cayenne pepper
4 garlic cloves, crushed
½ cup (15 g) chopped fresh
   flat-leaf parsley
½ cup (25 g) chopped fresh coriander
⅓ cup (80 ml) lemon juice
¼ cup (125 ml) olive oil

1 If using wooden skewers, soak them in water for 30 minutes to prevent burning. Place the tuna in a shallow non-metallic dish. Combine the olive oil, ground cumin and lemon rind, and pour over the tuna. Toss to coat and leave to marinate for 10 minutes.

2 To make the Chermoula, place the cumin, coriander, paprika and cayenne in a frying pan and cook over medium heat for 30 seconds, or until fragrant. Combine with the remaining ingredients and leave for the flavours to develop.

3 Thread the tuna onto the skewers. Lightly oil a chargrill or barbecue, and cook the skewers for 1 minute on each side for rare and 2 minutes for medium. Serve on couscous with the chermoula drizzled over the skewers.

Pour the combined olive oil, cumin and lemon rind over the tuna cubes.

Combine the chermoula ingredients in a small bowl.

Thread the tuna onto the skewers and grill until done to your liking.

INVOLTINI OF SWORDFISH

Preparation time: 30 minutes
Total cooking time: 10 minutes
Serves 4

1 kg swordfish, skin removed,
cut into four 5 cm pieces
3 lemons
⅓ cup (80 ml) olive oil
1 small onion, chopped
3 cloves garlic, chopped
2 tablespoons chopped capers
2 tablespoons chopped pitted
    Kalamata olives
¼ cup (35 g) finely grated parmesan
1½ cups (120 g) fresh breadcrumbs
2 tablespoons chopped fresh parsley
1 egg, lightly beaten
24 fresh bay leaves
2 small white onions, quartered and
    separated into pieces
2 tablespoons lemon juice, extra

1 Cut each swordfish piece horizontally into 4 slices to give you 16 slices. Place each piece between two pieces of plastic wrap and roll gently with a rolling pin to flatten without tearing. Cut each piece in half to give 32 pieces.
2 Peel the lemons with a vegetable peeler. Cut the peel into 24 even pieces. Juice the lemons to give 60 ml.
3 Heat 2 tablespoons olive oil, add the onion and garlic, and cook over medium heat for 2 minutes. Place in a bowl with the capers, olives, parmesan, breadcrumbs and parsley. Season, add the egg and mix to bind.
4 Divide the stuffing among the fish pieces and, with oiled hands, roll up to form parcels. Thread 4 rolls onto each of 8 skewers alternating with the bay leaves, lemon peel and onion.
5 Mix the remaining oil with the lemon juice in a small bowl. Barbecue or grill the skewers for 3–4 minutes each side, basting with the oil and lemon mixture. Serve the swordfish skewers with extra lemon juice drizzled over the top.

Roll the swordfish out between two pieces of plastic wrap.

Roll the fish pieces and filling up to form neat parcels.

Thread the rolls, bay leaves, lemon peel and onion onto skewers.

BARBECUED SCALLOPS ON GINGER AND SPINACH SALAD

Preparation time: 10 minutes
Total cooking time: 5 minutes
Serves 4

300 g fresh scallops, without roe
2 cups (100 g) baby English spinach
   leaves
1 small red capsicum, cut into very
   fine strips
50 g bean sprouts
25 ml sake
1 tablespoon lime juice
2 teaspoons shaved palm sugar
1 teaspoon fish sauce

1 Remove any veins, membrane or hard white muscle from the scallops. Lightly brush the barbecue or a chargrill plate with oil. Cook the scallops in batches on the barbecue or chargrill plate for 1 minute each side, or until cooked.

2 Divide the English spinach leaves, capsicum and bean sprouts among four serving plates. Arrange the scallops over the top.

3 To make the dressing, place the sake, lime juice, palm sugar and fish sauce in a small bowl, and mix together well. Pour over the salad and serve immediately.

COOK'S FILE

Note: Sprinkle with toasted sesame seeds, if desired.

BARBECUED CHERMOULA PRAWNS

Preparation time: 15 minutes
+ 10 minutes standing
Cooking time: 10 minutes
Serves 4

1 kg raw medium prawns
3 teaspoons hot paprika
2 teaspoons ground cumin
1 cup (30 g) firmly packed fresh
   flat-leaf parsley
½ cup (15 g) firmly packed fresh
   coriander leaves
100 ml lemon juice
145 ml olive oil
1½ cups (280 g) couscous
1 tablespoon grated lemon rind
lemon wedges, to serve

1 Peel the prawns, leaving the tails intact. Gently pull out the dark vein from the backs, starting at the head end. Place the prawns in a large bowl. Dry-fry the paprika and cumin in a frying pan for about 1 minute, or until fragrant. Remove from the heat.

2 Blend or process the spices, parsley, coriander, lemon juice and ½ cup (125 ml) of the oil until finely chopped. Add a little salt and pepper. Pour over the prawns and mix well, then cover with plastic wrap and refrigerate for 10 minutes. Heat a barbecue plate or chargrill pan to hot.

3 Meanwhile, to cook the couscous, bring 1 cup (250 ml) water to the boil in a saucepan, then stir in the couscous, lemon rind, the remaining oil and ¼ teaspoon salt. Remove from the heat, cover and leave for 5 minutes. Fluff the couscous with a fork, adding a little extra olive oil if needed.

4 Cook the prawns on a barbecue plate or chargrill pan for about 3–4 minutes, or until cooked through, turning and brushing with extra marinade while cooking (take care not to overcook). Serve the prawns on a bed of couscous, with a wedge of lemon.

1

CAJUN CALAMARI

Preparation time: 15 minutes
+ 3 hours marinating
Total cooking time: 5 minutes
Serves 4

600 g large calamari (or squid) hoods
¼ cup lemon juice
2 cloves garlic, crushed
2 teaspoons tomato paste
1 teaspoon garam masala
2 teaspoons ground coriander
2 teaspoons paprika
2 teaspoons seasoned pepper

2 teaspoons caster sugar
1 tablespoon grated fresh ginger
1 tablespoon olive oil
¼ teaspoon ground nutmeg
pinch chilli powder

1 Wash calamari thoroughly, removing any membrane. Pat dry with paper towel. Using a sharp knife, cut through one side of each hood, open out to give a large, flat piece of flesh. With inside facing up, score flesh diagonally, in a criss-cross pattern, taking care not to cut all the way through. Against the grain of those cuts, slice flesh into long strips about 2 cm thick.

2 Combine juice, garlic, tomato paste, spices, sugar, ginger, oil, nutmeg and chilli in bowl; mix well. Add calamari strips; stir to combine. Cover and refrigerate several hours or overnight. Prepare and heat barbecue 1 hour before cooking.

3 Cook calamari and marinade on hot lightly greased barbecue flatplate 5 minutes or until flesh curls and turns white. Remove from the heat and serve immediately.

COOK'S FILE
Storage time: Calamari can be marinated up to 2 days in advance.

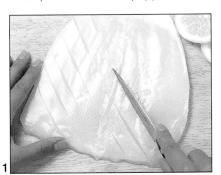

1

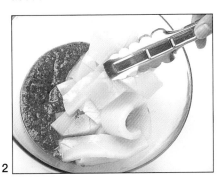

2

3

BLACKENED FISH WITH PINEAPPLE SALSA

Preparation time: 15 minutes
+ 20 minutes refrigeration
Total cooking time: 15 minutes
Serves 6

8 cm piece fresh pineapple, finely
    diced
6 spring onions, thinly sliced
2 tablespoons finely shredded fresh
    mint
¼ cup (60 ml) coconut
    vinegar
¼ cup (60 ml) olive oil
6 tablespoons ready-made Cajun
    spices
6 ling fillets
½ cup (60 g) Greek-style plain
    yoghurt

1 Place the pineapple, spring onion and mint in a bowl. Season with pepper and mix together well. Just before serving, stir in the vinegar and 2 tablespoons of the oil, and stir.
2 Place the Cajun spices in a dry frying pan and dry-fry over medium heat for 1 minute, or until fragrant. Transfer the spices to a sheet of baking paper and lightly coat each side of the fish fillets, patting off any excess. Refrigerate for 20 minutes.
3 Heat a barbecue or chargrill plate and lightly brush with the remaining oil. Cook the fish in 2 batches for 2–3 minutes on each side, depending on the thickness of the fish. Serve with a little yoghurt spooned over the top and the salsa on the side.

GRILLED CALAMARI WITH SALSA VERDE

Preparation time: 30 minutes
+ 30 minutes marinating
Total cooking time: 15 minutes
Serves 4

1 kg calamari
1 cup (250 ml) olive oil
2 tablespoons lemon juice
2 cloves garlic, crushed
2 tablespoons chopped fresh oregano
2 tablespoons chopped fresh
    flat-leaf parsley
6 lemon wedges

SALSA VERDE
2 anchovy fillets, drained
1 tablespoon capers
1 clove garlic, crushed
2 tablespoons chopped fresh
    flat-leaf parsley
2 tablespoons olive oil

1 To clean the calamari, hold onto the hood and gently pull the tentacles away from the head. Cut out the beak and discard with any intestines still attached to the tentacles. Rinse the tentacles in cold running water, pat dry and cut into 5 cm lengths. Place in a bowl. Clean out the hood cavity and remove the transparent backbone. Under cold running water, pull away the skin, rinse and dry well. Cut into 1 cm rings and place in the bowl with the tentacles. Add the oil, lemon juice, garlic and oregano to the bowl, and toss to coat the calamari. Refrigerate for 30 minutes.

2 To make the Salsa Verde, crush the anchovy fillets in a mortar and pestle or in a bowl with a wooden spoon.

Rinse the capers and dry with paper towels. Chop the capers very finely and add to the anchovies. Add the garlic and parsley, then slowly stir in the olive oil. Season with black pepper and salt, if necessary (the anchovies may be very salty). Mix well.

3 Drain the calamari and cook on a hot barbecue or grill in 4 batches for 1–2 minutes each side, basting with the marinade. To serve, sprinkle the calamari with salt, pepper and fresh parsley, and serve with the Salsa Verde and lemon wedges.

Hold the calamari and gently pull the tentacles away from the head.

Combine the anchovies, capers, garlic and parsley.

Cook the calamari in batches on a hot barbecue or grill.

SWEET AND SOUR FISH KEBABS

Preparation time: 20 minutes
+ 3 hours marinating
Total cooking time: 10 minutes
Makes 12 skewers

750 g boneless white fish fillets (hake or cod)
225 g can pineapple pieces
1 large red capsicum
3 teaspoons soy sauce
6 teaspoons soft brown sugar
2 tablespoons white vinegar
2 tablespoons tomato sauce
salt, to taste

1 Soak wooden skewers in water for several hours. Cut fish into 2.5 cm cubes. Drain pineapple, reserving 2 tablespoons liquid. Cut capsicum into 2.5 cm pieces. Thread capsicum, fish and pineapple alternately onto skewers.

2 Place kebabs in shallow non-metal dish. Combine soy sauce, reserved pineapple juice, sugar, vinegar, tomato sauce and salt in small bowl; mix well. Pour marinade over kebabs. Cover; refrigerate several hours. Prepare and heat barbecue 1 hour before cooking.

3 Barbecue kebabs on hot lightly grease flatplate, brushing frequently with marinade, 2–3 minutes each side or until just cooked through. Serve immediately with cooked noodles and a dressed green salad, if desired.

COOK'S FILE

Storage time: Kebabs are best cooked just before serving. Do not marinate longer than 3 hours.

1

2

3

SWEET CHILLI OCTOPUS

Preparation time: 15 minutes
Total cooking time: 5 minutes
Serves 4

1.5 kg baby octopus
1 cup (250 ml) sweet chilli sauce
⅓ cup (80 ml) lime juice
⅓ cup (80 ml) fish sauce
½ cup (60 g) soft brown sugar
oil, for chargrilling
200 g mixed salad leaves, to serve
lime wedges, to serve

1 Cut the head from the octopus and discard. With your fingers, push the hard beak up and out of the body. Rinse under cold water, drain and pat dry.

2 Place the sweet chilli sauce, lime juice, fish sauce and sugar in a small bowl and mix together well.

3 Brush a barbecue or chargrill plate with oil and heat to very hot. Cook the octopus, turning, for 3–4 minutes, or until they change colour. Brush with a quarter of the sauce during cooking. Do not overcook. Serve immediately on a bed of salad greens with the remaining sauce and the lime wedges.

DILL FISH WITH LEMON BUTTER SAUCE

Preparation time: 10 minutes
+ 3 hours marinating
Total cooking time: 10 minutes
Serves 4

4 boneless white fish fillets (perch or whiting)
6 teaspoons lemon pepper
1–2 tablespoons chopped fresh dill
1/3 cup lemon juice

LEMON BUTTER SAUCE

2 tablespoons lemon juice
1/2 cup cream
40 g butter, chopped
2 tablespoons chopped fresh chives

1 Rinse fish under cold water. Sprinkle pepper all over fillets and place in shallow non-metal dish. Combine dill and lemon juice. Pour over fish, cover and refrigerate several hours. Prepare and heat barbecue 1 hour before cooking.
2 Cook the fish on hot lightly greased barbecue flatplate for 2–3 minutes each side or until flesh flakes back easily with a fork. Serve with the Lemon Butter Sauce, barbecued citrus slices and a green salad, if desired.
3 To make Lemon Butter Sauce, simmer lemon juice in a small pan until reduced by half. Add cream; stir until mixed through. Whisk in butter a little at a time until all the butter has melted; stir in chives.

COOK'S FILE

Storage time: The fish and sauce are best cooked just before serving.

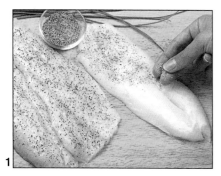

TUNA WITH CAPONATA

Preparation time: 25 minutes
+ 1 hour standing + cooling
Total cooking time: 50 minutes
Serves 6

CAPONATA

500 g ripe tomatoes
750 g eggplant, cut into 1 cm cubes
1/3 cup (80 ml) olive oil
2 tablespoons olive oil, extra
1 onion, chopped
3 celery sticks, chopped
2 tablespoons drained capers
1/2 cup (90 g) green olives, pitted
1 tablespoon sugar
1/2 cup (125 ml) red wine vinegar

olive oil, for brushing
6 x 200 g tuna steaks

1 To make the Caponata, score a cross in the base of each tomato. Place in a bowl of boiling water for 1 minute, then plunge into cold water and peel away from the cross. Cut into 1 cm cubes.
2 Sprinkle the eggplant with salt and leave for 1 hour. Place in a colander, rinse under cold running water and pat dry. Heat half the oil in a frying pan, add half the eggplant and cook for 4–5 minutes, or until golden and soft. Remove. Repeat with the remaining oil and eggplant. Remove.
3 Heat the extra oil in the same pan, add the onion and celery, and cook for 3–4 minutes, or until golden. Reduce the heat to low, add the tomato and simmer for 15 minutes, stirring occasionally. Stir in the capers, olives, sugar and vinegar, season and

simmer, stirring occasionally, for 10 minutes, or until slightly reduced. Stir in the eggplant. Remove from the heat and cool.
4 Heat a barbecue or chargrill plate and brush lightly with olive oil. Cook the tuna for 2–3 minutes each side,

or until cooked to your liking. Serve the tuna immediately with the Caponata.

Cook the eggplant in two batches until golden and soft.

Add the capers, olives, sugar and vinegar to the tomato mixture.

Cook the tuna on a chargrill plate until cooked to your liking.

93

BARBECUED LOBSTER TAILS WITH AVOCADO SAUCE

Preparation time: 15 minutes
+ 3 hours marinating
Total cooking time: 10 minutes
Serves 4

¼ cup dry white wine
1 tablespoon honey
1 teaspoon sambal oelek (bottled chopped chillies)
1 clove garlic, crushed
1 tablespoon olive oil
4 (400 g) fresh green lobster tails

AVOCADO SAUCE
1 medium ripe avocado, mashed
3 teaspoons lemon juice
2 tablespoons sour cream
1 small tomato, chopped finely
salt and pepper, to taste

1 Combine wine, honey, sambal oelek, garlic and oil in jug; mix well. Use a sharp knife or kitchen scissors to cut along the soft shell on the underside of the lobster. Gently pull shell apart and ease raw flesh out with fingers.
2 Place lobster in shallow non-metal dish. Pour over marinade; stir well. Cover, refrigerate several hours or overnight. Prepare and light barbecue 1 hour before cooking. Cook lobster tails on hot lightly greased barbecue grill or flatplate 5–10 minutes, turning frequently. Brush with marinade until cooked through. Slice into medallions and serve with Avocado Sauce and a green salad, if desired.
3 To make Avocado Sauce, combine avocado, juice and sour cream in bowl; mix well. Add tomato and combine with avocado mixture; add salt and pepper, to taste.

COOK'S FILE

Storage time: Avocado Sauce can be made 2–3 hours ahead. Before refrigerating, press plastic wrap onto surface; this will prevent it turning black.

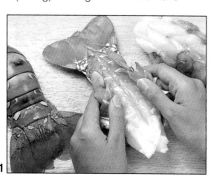

MEDITERRANEAN SWORDFISH WITH WHITE BEAN PURÉE

Preparation time: 25 minutes
+ 30 minutes soaking + 30
minutes marinating
Total cooking time: 20 minutes
Serves 4

1 kg swordfish steaks, cut into
  3 cm cubes
1 tablespoon olive oil
2 tablespoons lemon juice
1 clove garlic, crushed
1 tablespoon chopped fresh rosemary
1 tablespoon chopped fresh thyme
2 tablespoons chopped fresh
  flat-leaf parsley

WHITE BEAN PURÉE
2 x 400 g cans cannellini beans
1½ cups (375 ml) chicken stock
2 fresh bay leaves
2 cloves garlic, crushed
1 teaspoon chopped fresh thyme
½ teaspoon finely grated lemon rind
¼ cup (60 ml) extra virgin olive oil

1 Soak eight wooden skewers in water for at least 30 minutes to prevent them from burning during cooking. Thread the swordfish cubes onto the skewers. Place in a large non-metallic dish and pour on the combined olive oil, lemon juice, garlic, rosemary and thyme. Season well. Cover with plastic wrap and refrigerate for at least 30 minutes.

2 Meanwhile, to make the white bean purée, wash the beans in a colander and place in a large saucepan. Add the chicken stock, bay leaves and ½ cup (125 ml) water. Bring to the boil, then reduce the heat and simmer for 10 minutes. Remove from the heat and drain well, reserving 2 tablespoons of the liquid.

3 Place the beans and the reserved liquid in a food processor or blender with the garlic, thyme and lemon rind. Season with salt and pepper and process until smooth. With the motor running, gradually pour in the olive oil in a thin stream. Continue processing until well combined, then keep warm.

4 Heat a barbecue or chargrill plate until very hot. Cook the skewers, turning regularly and basting with any leftover marinade, for 3–4 minutes, or until cooked through and golden.

5 Serve the skewers warm, sprinkled with parsley and a spoonful of white bean purée on the side.

Drain the beans over a heatproof bowl and reserve some of the liquid.

Process the beans, garlic, thyme and lemon rind, then the oil, in a food processor.

Chargrill the swordfish skewers until cooked through and golden.

SAUCES FOR SEAFOOD

These sauces and salsas are the perfect accompaniment for barbecued fish or other seafood. Leftovers can be refrigerated in an airtight container for up to three days.

SALSA VERDE
Place 1 cup (20 g) tightly packed fresh flat-leaf parsley, 1 clove crushed garlic, 3 tablespoons fresh dill, 2 tablespoons chopped chives and 4 tablespoons fresh mint in a food processor and process for 30 seconds, or until combined. Add 1 tablespoon lemon juice, 5 anchovy fillets and 3 tablespoons drained, bottled capers and process until mixed. With the motor running, slowly add ½ cup (125 ml) olive oil in a thin stream and process until all the oil is added and the mixture is smooth. Serve with grilled prawns or fish kebabs (e.g. swordfish or salmon). Serves 4.

BUTTER SAUCE
Finely chop two French shallots and place in a small saucepan with ¼ cup (60 ml) each of white wine vinegar and water. Bring to the boil, then reduce the heat and simmer until reduced to 2 tablespoons. Remove from the heat and strain into a clean saucepan. Return to the heat and whisk in 220 g cubed unsalted butter, a few pieces at a time. The sauce will thicken as the butter is added. Season, to taste, with salt, pepper and lemon juice. Serve with poached fish fillets such as salmon or barramundi, or char-grilled lobster tail. Serves 4–6.

CANNELLINI BEAN AND SEMI-DRIED TOMATO SALSA
Drain a 400 g can cannellini beans and rinse the beans. Put in a bowl and stir with ½ cup (75 g) chopped semi-dried tomatoes, ¼ cup (30 g) sliced pitted black olives and ¼ red onion, chopped. Stir in 1 tablespoon olive oil, 3 teaspoons white wine vinegar and 1 tablespoon finely chopped fresh flat-leaf parsley. Cover and refrigerate for 30 minutes, or until required. Serve with fish such as baked red mullet or snapper. Serves 6.

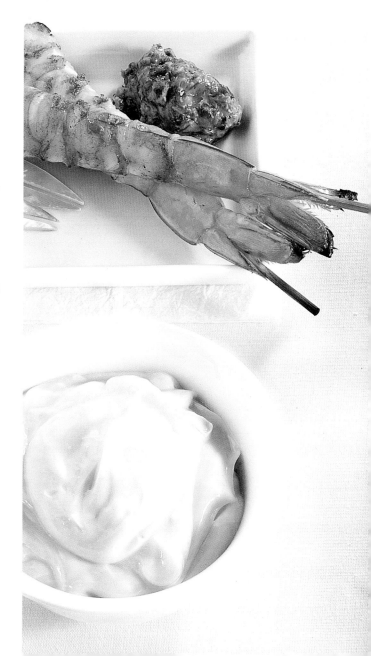

ROASTED CAPSICUM AND BASIL SAUCE

Preheat the oven to hot 210°C (415°F/Gas 6–7). Halve two red capsicums and place skin-side-up on a greased baking tray with two cloves unpeeled garlic. Brush with olive oil and bake for 20 minutes, or until the capsicum is soft and the skin is blackened and blistered. Remove and cool the capsicums in a plastic bag. Peel the capsicums and garlic and mix in a food processor or blender for 30 seconds, or until combined. With the motor running, slowly add 100 ml olive oil in a thin stream and blend until all the oil is added and the mixture is smooth. Add 1 tablespoon finely chopped fresh basil, ¼ teaspoon salt and freshly ground black pepper. Serve warm or cold with char-grilled fish such as sardines, swordfish or tuna. Serves 4.

CREAMY TARRAGON SAUCE

Combine ½ cup (125 ml) fish stock in a small saucepan with 1 crushed clove garlic, 1 teaspoon dried tarragon leaves and 1 thinly sliced spring onion. Bring to the boil, then reduce the heat and simmer for 3 minutes, or until reduced by half. Add 1 cup (250 ml) thick cream or mascarpone. Reduce the heat to very low and stir until the cream has fully melted. Add ½ teaspoon lemon juice, 2 tablespoons grated parmesan and salt and ground black pepper, to taste. Simmer for 1 minute, then serve with grilled fish cutlets such as blue-eye. Serves 4–6.

MANGO AVOCADO SALSA

Cut 1 mango and 1 avocado into 1 cm cubes and place in a small bowl with 1 diced small red capsicum. Mix 2 tablespoons lime juice with 1 teaspoon caster sugar in a jug and pour over the mango. Stir in 3 tablespoons chopped fresh coriander leaves. Serve with chilled cooked seafood such as prawns or smoked salmon. Serves 6.

WEBER/ KETTLE COOKERY

ORANGE AND GINGER GLAZED HAM

Preparation time: 25 minutes
Total cooking time: 1 hour
30 minutes
Serves 20

6 kg ham on the bone
¼ cup orange juice
¾ cup orange marmalade
1 tablespoon grated ginger
2 teaspoons mustard powder
2 tablespoons soft brown sugar
whole cloves (about 30)

1 Prepare the weber (kettle) barbecue for indirect cooking at moderate heat (normal fire). Remove the rind by running your thumb around edge of ham, under the rind. Begin pulling from the widest edge. When rind has been removed to within 10 cm of the shank end, cut through the rind around the shank. Using a sharp knife, remove excess fat from ham; discard fat. (Reserve rind for crackling, if desired. Rub rind with salt and barbecue for 40 minutes.)

2 Using a sharp knife score the top of ham with deep diagonal cuts. Score diagonally the other way, forming a diamond pattern. Place ham on barbecue; put lid on barbecue and cook 45 minutes.

3 Place juice, marmalade, ginger, mustard and sugar in small pan. Stir over medium heat until comb-ined; set aside to cool. Remove lid from barbecue; carefully press cloves into top of ham (approximately one clove per diamond); brush all over with the marmalade mixture. Cover barbecue, cook a further 45 minutes. Serve garnished with clove-studded orange slices. The ham can be served warm or cold.

COOK'S FILE

Storage time: Cover ham with a clean, dry cloth; store in refrigeratorfor up to 1 month. Change the cloth every 2–3 days.
Note: Leftover ham, cubed, is delicious in fried rice. Use the ham bone for stock or as the basis of pea soup.

WHOLE FILLET OF BEEF WITH MUSTARD COATING

Preparation time: 1 hour
5 minutes
+ 15 minutes standing
Total cooking time: 40 minutes
Serves 6–8

2 kg scotch fillet of beef
¼ cup brandy

MUSTARD COATING
⅓ cup wholegrain mustard
¼ cup cream
¾ teaspoon black pepper, coarsely
   ground

1 Prepare weber (kettle) barbecue for indirect cooking at moderate heat (normal fire). Trim meat of excess fat and sinew. Tie meat securely with string at regular intervals to retain its shape. Brush beef all over with the brandy; allow to stand for 1 hour.
2 To make Mustard Coating, combine mustard, cream and pepper in small bowl. Spread evenly over top and sides of fillet.
3 Place meat on large greased sheet of foil. Grasp corners of foil and pinch securely to form a tray. (This will hold in the juices). Place lid on barbecue and cook 30–40 minutes for medium-rare meat. Stand 10–15 minutes then carve into thick slices. Serve warm with barbecued or grilled vegetables.

COOK'S FILE

Storage time: Beef can be marinated in brandy up to 1 day in advance. Store, covered, in refrigerator.
Hint: Reserve cooking juices left in foil to make a gravy; stir in a tablespoon of prepared mustard.

WEBER CHICKEN

Preparation time: 10 minutes
Total cooking time: 1 hour 30
minutes
Serves 4–6

1.8 kg chicken
salt
½ teaspoon cracked peppercorns
1 whole head garlic
small bunch fresh oregano
¼ cup olive oil

1 Prepare weber (kettle) barbecue for indirect cooking at medium heat (normal fire). Place a drip tray underneath top grill. Remove giblets and any large fat deposits from chicken. Wipe chicken and pat dry with paper towel. Season chicken cavity with salt and pepper.
Using a sharp knife, cut off top of head of garlic. Push the whole head of garlic, unpeeled, into the cavity. Follow with whole bunch of oregano. Close cavity with several toothpicks or a skewer.
2 Rub chicken skin with salt and brush with oil. Place on barbecue over drip tray. Put lid on barbecue and cook 1 hour, brushing occasionally with olive oil to keep the skin moist. Insert skewer into chicken thigh. If juices run clear chicken is cooked through. Stand chicken away from heat 5 minutes before carving.
3 Carefully separate garlic cloves; serve 1 or 2 cloves with each serving of chicken. (The flesh can be squeezed from the clove and eaten with chicken.)

COOK'S FILE

Storage time: Chicken is best cooked close to serving. Chicken can be kept warm in the barbecue; open top and bottom vents to prevent further cooking.
Hint: Toast slices of French bread and spread with the cooked garlic; add a drizzle of olive oil, salt and pepper. Serve with the chicken or mix through a salad.

1

3

SMOKED CHICKEN FILLETS

Preparation time: 5 minutes
Total cooking time: 25 minutes
Serves 4

4 chicken breast
fillets (1 kg)

1 tablespoon olive oil
seasoned pepper, to taste
hickory or mesquite chips, for
   smoking

1 Prepare weber (kettle) barbecue for indirect cooking at moderate heat (normal fire). Trim chicken of excess fat and sinew. Brush the chicken with oil and sprinkle over the seasoned pepper.

2 Spoon a pile of smoking chips (about 25) over the coals in each charcoal rail.
3 Cover barbecue and cook chicken 15 minutes. Test with a sharp knife. If juices do not run clear cook another 5–10 minutes until cooked as desired. Serve with chilli noodles, if liked.

1

2

3

BARBECUED LAMB SHANKS

Preparation time: 5 minutes
+ overnight marinating
Total cooking time: 45 minutes
Serves 6

2 cloves garlic, halved
1/3 cup olive oil
6 lamb shanks
salt and pepper, to taste

1 Combine garlic and oil in small bowl, cover and marinate at room temperature overnight. Prepare weber (kettle) barbecue for indirect cooking at moderate heat (normal fire). Place drip tray under top grill. Trim off any excess fat and sinew.
2 Brush the garlic oil generously over the shanks and sprinkle with salt and pepper.
3 Place lamb shanks on the top grill of the barbecue, cover with lid and roast 35–45 minutes or until the meat is tender when pierced with a fork. Serve with barbecued vegetables, such as capsicum, and thick slices of chargrilled potato, scattered with herbs, if desired.

COOK'S FILE

Storage time: Lamb shanks can be marinated and stored in refrigerator 1 day in advance.
Hint: For a more intense flavour, double the quantity of garlic in the oil and brush over lamb several hours before cooking. Pour remaining garlic oil over shanks before serving.
Variation: Try this recipe with other boned cuts of meat, such as lamb neck chops, osso bucco, pieces of ox tail and chicken drumsticks.

LEG OF LAMB

Preparation time: 15 minutes
Total cooking time: 1 hour
30 minutes
Serves 6

2 kg leg of lamb
4 cloves garlic
6–8 sprigs rosemary
2 tablespoons olive oil

2 tablespoons freshly ground black pepper

1 Prepare the weber (kettle) barbecue for indirect cooking at moderate heat (normal fire). Place a drip tray on the bottom grill. Trim meat of excess fat and sinew. Cut narrow, deep slits all over top and sides of the meat.
2 Cut the garlic cloves in half lengthways. Push the garlic and rosemary sprigs into slits. Brush all over with oil and sprinkle with black pepper.
3 Place lamb on barbecue grill over drip tray, cover and cook for 1 hour 30 minutes for medium-rare meat. Brush with olive oil occasionally. Stand lamb in a warm place, covered with foil, 10–15 minutes before carving.

COOK'S FILE

Storage time: Barbecue lamb just before serving.

BAKED VEGETABLES

Preparation time: 20 minutes
Total cooking time: 1 hour
15 minutes
Serves 6

6 medium potatoes
60 g butter, melted
1/4 teaspoon paprika
750 g pumpkin
6 small onions
150 g green beans
150 g broccoli
20 g butter, chopped, extra

1 Prepare weber (kettle) barbecue for indirect cooking at moderate heat (normal fire). Peel potatoes and cut in half. Using a small, sharp knife, make deep, fine cuts into potato, taking care not to cut all the way through. Take two large sheets of aluminium foil, fold in half and brush liberally with some melted butter. Place the potatoes unscored-side down on foil and fold up edges of foil to create a tray. Brush the potatoes with melted butter and sprinkle with paprika.
2 Cut pumpkin into three wedges, cut each wedge in half. Peel onions and trim bases slightly, so they will sit flat on grill. Brush pumpkin and onions with melted butter. Place tray of potatoes, pumpkin pieces and onions on barbecue grill. Put lid on barbecue; cook 1 hour.
3 Top and tail beans; cut broccoli into florets. Place on a sheet of foil brushed with melted butter. Dot with extra butter; enclose in foil. Add to other vegetables on grill, cook a further 15 minutes.

COOK'S FILE

Storage time: Vegetables are best cooked just before serving.
Hint: If barbecuing chicken or lamb, cook vegetables simultaneously, timing them to be ready with the meat. If vegeta-bles are cooked early, wrap in foil and store in a warm place until needed.
Variation: Use any of your favourite vegetables for this recipe. Hard vegetables (turnips and sweet potatoes) can be placed directly on the grill. Cook small or leafy vegetables (mushrooms, spinach or asparagus) in foil parcels. Cooking times are the same as for a conventional oven.

*Leg of Lamb
with Baked Vegetables.*

WHOLE FISH WITH LEMON HERB BUTTER

Preparation time: 15 minutes
Total cooking time: 1 hour
Serves 4

2 kg whole white-fleshed fish

HERB BUTTER
80 g butter, softened
1 tablespoon chopped parsley
3 teaspoons thyme leaves
1 tablespoon chopped chives
2 teaspoons grated lemon rind
1 small lemon, sliced

1 Prepare weber (kettle) barbecue for indirect cooking at moderate heat (normal fire). Wash and scale fish; pat dry with a paper towel. Place fish on a large sheet of oiled aluminium foil.

2 To make Herb Butter, blend butter, herbs and lemon rind in a small bowl; beat until smooth. Spread half of the butter mixture inside the cavity of the fish. Transfer the remaining butter mixture to a serving bowl.

3 Lay lemon slices over the fish, enclose fish in foil and place on barbecue grill. Cover, cook 1 hour or until flesh flakes easily with a fork. Serve with extra Herb Butter.

COOK'S FILE

Storage time: Herb Butter can be made up to 2 weeks in advance, provided it is well covered and refrigerated. Fish is best cooked just before serving.
Note: Leftover Herb Butter can be spread on hot bread, or served with cooked vegetables or meats such as steak and chicken.

1

2

3

SPICED SWEET POTATOES

Preparation time: 20 minutes
Total cooking time: 25 minutes
Serves 4–6

500 g orange sweet potatoes
¼ cup demerara sugar

¾ teaspoon mixed spice
30 g butter, chopped
⅓ cup orange juice

1 Prepare weber (kettle) barbecue for indirect cooking at moderate heat (normal fire). Peel sweet potatoes and cut into thick slices. Arrange in layers in shallow greased tray. Sprinkle over combined sugar and mixed spice; dot with butter.

2 Sprinkle over the orange juice.
3 Cover tray with foil, place on top grill of barbecue, replace lid, cook 20 minutes. Lift foil and test with a sharp knife; if needed, cook a few more minutes. Sprinkle on a little orange juice if potatoes get dry.

COOK'S FILE

Storage time: This dish is best cooked just before serving.

1

2

3

VEGETABLES AND SALADS

MARINATED GRILLED VEGETABLES

Preparation time: 30 minutes
+ 1 hour marinating
Total cooking time: 5 minutes
Serves 6

3 small slender eggplant
2 small red capsicum
3 medium zucchini
6 medium mushrooms

MARINADE
¼ cup olive oil
¼ cup lemon juice
¼ cup shredded fresh basil
1 clove garlic, crushed

1 Cut the eggplant into diagonal slices. Place on tray in single layer; sprinkle with salt and let it stand 15 minutes. Rinse thoroughly and pat dry with paper towels. Trim capsicum, removing seeds and membrane; cut the capsicum into long, wide pieces. Cut the zucchini into diagonal slices. Trim each mushroom stalk so that it is level with the cap. Place all the vegetables in a large, shallow non-metal dish.

2 To make Marinade, place oil, juice, basil and garlic in a small screwtop jar. Shake vigorously to combine. Pour over vegetables and combine well. Store, covered with plastic wrap, in refrigerator for 1 hour, stirring occasionally. Prepare and heat barbecue.

3 Place vegetables on hot, lightly greased barbecue grill or flatplate. Cook each vegetable piece over the hottest part of the fire 2 minutes each side. Transfer to a serving dish once browned. Brush vegetables frequently with any remaining marinade while cooking.

COOK'S FILE

Storage time: Vegetables can be marinated up to 2 hours before cooking. Take vegetables out of the refrigerator 15 minutes before cooking to allow oil in the marinade to soften.
Hint: The vegetables can be served warm or cold. Serve leftovers with thick slices of crusty bread or rolls. Other herbs, such as parsley, rosemary or thyme, can be added to the marinade. The marinade can also be used as a salad dressing. Store extra marinade for dressing in a screwtop jar in the refrigerator for up to 2 weeks. Olive oil solidifies when cold, so let the marinade come to room temperature before use.

VEGETABLE SKEWERS WITH BASIL COUSCOUS

Preparation time: 15 minutes
+ 30 minutes soaking
+ 10 minutes standing
Cooking time: 15 minutes
Serves 4

5 thin zucchini, cut into 2 cm cubes
5 slender eggplants, cut into 2 cm cubes
12 button mushrooms, halved
2 red capsicums, cut into 1.5 cm cubes
250 g kefalotyri cheese, cut into 2 cm thick pieces (see Note)
⅓ cup (80 ml) lemon juice
2 garlic cloves, finely chopped
5 tablespoons finely chopped fresh basil
145 ml extra virgin olive oil
1 cup (185 g) couscous
1 teaspoon grated lemon rind

1 Soak 12 wooden skewers in water for 30 minutes to prevent them burning during cooking. Thread alternate pieces of vegetables and kefalotyri, starting and finishing with a piece of capsicum and using two pieces of kefalotyri per skewer. Place in a non-metallic dish large enough to hold them in one layer.
2 Combine the lemon juice, garlic, 4 tablespoons of the basil and ½ cup (125 ml) of the oil in a non-metallic bowl. Season. Pour two thirds of the marinade over the skewers, reserving the remainder. Turn the skewers to coat evenly, cover with plastic wrap and marinate for at least 5 minutes.
3 Place the couscous, lemon rind and 1½ cups (375 ml) boiling water in a large heatproof bowl. Stand for 5 minutes, or until all the water has been absorbed. Add the remaining oil and basil, then fluff gently with a fork to separate the grains. Cover.
4 Meanwhile, heat a barbecue plate or chargrill pan to medium–high.

Cook the skewers, brushing often with the leftover marinade in the non-metallic dish, for 4–5 minutes on each side, or until the vegetables are cooked and the cheese browns—take care that the cheese doesn't fall apart during cooking.
5 Divide the couscous and skewers among four serving plates. Season, then drizzle with the reserved marinade to taste. Serve immediately with lemon wedges, if desired.

COOK'S FILE

Note: Kefalotyri can be found in continental delicatessens and in some larger supermarkets. If not available, use haloumi instead.

MUSHROOM AND EGGPLANT SKEWERS WITH TOMATO CONCASSE

Preparation time: 20 minutes
+ 15 minutes marinating
Total cooking time: 25 minutes
Serves 4

12 long rosemary sprigs
18 Swiss brown mushrooms
1 eggplant, cut into 2 cm cubes
¼ cup (60 ml) olive oil
2 tablespoons balsamic vinegar
2 cloves garlic, crushed
1 teaspoon sugar
olive oil, for brushing
sea salt, to sprinkle (optional)

TOMATO CONCASSÉ

5 tomatoes
1 tablespoon olive oil
1 small onion, finely chopped
1 clove garlic, crushed
1 tablespoon tomato paste
2 teaspoons sugar
2 teaspoons balsamic vinegar
1 tablespoon chopped flat-leaf parsley

1 Remove the leaves from the rosemary sprigs, leaving 5 cm on the tip. Reserve 1 tablespoon of the leaves. Cut the mushrooms in half, keeping the stems intact. Place the mushrooms and eggplant in a large non-metallic bowl. Pour on the combined oil, vinegar, garlic and sugar, then season and toss. Marinate for 15 minutes.
2 Score a cross in the base of each tomato. Put in a bowl of boiling water for 30 seconds then plunge into cold water. Peel the skin away from the cross. Cut in half and scoop out the seeds with a teaspoon. Dice.
3 Heat the oil in a saucepan. Cook the onion and garlic over a medium

heat for 2–3 minutes, or until soft. Reduce the heat, add the tomato, tomato paste, sugar, vinegar and parsley and simmer for 10 minutes, or until the liquid has evaporated. Keep warm.
4 Thread alternating mushroom halves and eggplant cubes onto the rosemary sprigs, so each sprig has three mushroom halves and two cubes of eggplant. Lightly oil a chargrill plate or barbecue and cook the skewers for 7–8 minutes, or until the eggplant is tender, turning occasionally. Serve with concassé and sprinkle with sea salt and the reserved rosemary.

Simmer the tomato sauce until it is thick and pulpy.

Thread alternating mushrooms and eggplant cubes onto the skewers.

111

GRILLED HALOUMI AND ROAST VEGETABLE SALAD

Preparation time: 15 minutes
Total cooking time: 30 minutes
Serves 4

4 slender eggplants, cut in half, halved lengthways
1 red capsicum, halved, thickly sliced
4 small zucchini, cut in half, halved lengthways
⅓ cup (80 ml) olive oil
2 cloves garlic, crushed
200 g haloumi cheese, cut into 5 mm thick slices
150 g baby English spinach leaves, trimmed
1 tablespoon balsamic vinegar

1 Preheat the oven to hot 220°C (425°F/Gas 7). Place the vegetables in a large bowl, add ¼ cup (60 ml) olive oil and the garlic, season and toss well to combine. Place the vegetables in an ovenproof dish in a single layer and roast for 20–30 minutes, or until tender and browned around the edges.
2 Meanwhile, lightly brush a barbecue, chargrill or heavy-based frying pan with oil and cook the haloumi slices for 1–2 minutes on each side.
3 Place the spinach leaves on four serving plates. Top with the roast vegetables and haloumi. Place the remaining oil in a small jug, add the vinegar and whisk to combine, then pour over the vegetables and haloumi. Serve immediately warm or at room temperature with lots of crusty bread.

COOK'S FILE

Note: You can use any roasted vegetable, such as orange sweet potatoes, leeks and Roma tomatoes.

1

2

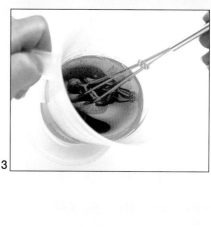

3

TOFU KEBABS WITH ASIAN MISO PESTO

Preparation time: 30 minutes
+ 1 hour marinating
Total cooking time: 10 minutes
Serves 4

1 large red capsicum, cut into squares
12 button mushrooms, halved
6 pickling onions, quartered
3 zucchini, cut into 3 cm chunks
450 g firm tofu, cut into 2 cm cubes
½ cup (125 ml) light olive oil
¼ cup (60 ml) light soy sauce
2 cloves garlic, crushed
2 teaspoons grated fresh ginger

MISO PESTO
½ cup (80 g) unsalted roasted
   peanuts
2 cups (60 g) firmly packed fresh
   coriander leaves
2 tablespoons white miso paste
2 cloves garlic
100 ml olive oil

1 Soak 12 wooden skewers in cold water for 10 minutes. Thread the vegetable pieces and tofu alternately onto the skewers, then place in a large rectangular ceramic dish.
2 Combine the olive oil, soy sauce, garlic and ginger in a bowl, then pour half the mixture over the kebabs. Cover with plastic wrap and marinate for 1 hour.

3 To make the Miso Pesto, finely chop the peanuts, coriander leaves, miso paste and garlic in a food processor. Slowly add the olive oil while the machine is still running and blend until a smooth paste.
4 Heat a barbecue or grill plate and cook the kebabs, turning and brushing frequently with the rest of the marinade, for 4–6 minutes, or until the edges are slightly brown. Serve with steamed rice and a little of the Miso Pesto.

Thread the vegetable pieces and tofu cubes alternately onto the skewers.

Mix the nuts, coriander leaves, miso and garlic until finely chopped.

Brush the kebabs with the remaining marinade during cooking.

113

BABY BARBECUED POTATOES

Preparation time: 20 minutes
+ 1 hour standing
Total cooking time: 20 minutes
Serves 6

750 g baby potatoes
2 tablespoons olive oil
2 tablespoons fresh thyme leaves
2 teaspoons crushed sea salt

1 Wash potatoes thoroughly under cold water. Cut any large potatoes in half so that all potatoes are a uniform size for even cooking. Boil, steam or microwave potatoes until just tender. (Potatoes should remain whole and intact.) Drain and lightly dry with paper towels.

2 Place potatoes in large mixing bowl; add oil and thyme. Toss gently to coat potatoes, stand for 1 hour. Prepare and heat barbecue.

3 Place potatoes on hot, lightly greased barbecue flatplate. Cook

15 minutes, turning frequently and brushing with remaining oil and thyme mixture, until golden brown. Place in serving bowl and sprinkle with salt. Garnish with extra thyme sprigs, if desired.

COOK'S FILE

Storage time: Potatoes can be cooked and marinated 2 hours in advance. Barbecue just before serving.

Note: Sea salt is a pure form of salt that comes in large crystals. Table salt can be substituted.

1

2

3

BARBECUED CORN ON THE COB WITH TOMATO RELISH

Preparation time: 15 minutes
Total cooking time: 1 hour
Serves 6

6 large cobs fresh corn
1–2 tablespoons olive oil or
    vegetable oil
60 g butter
salt to taste

TOMATO RELISH

400 g can peeled tomatoes
$^2/_3$ cup white vinegar
$^1/_2$ cup white sugar
1 clove garlic, finely chopped
2 spring onions, finely chopped
4 sun-dried tomatoes, finely chopped
1 small fresh red chilli, finely chopped
$^1/_2$ teaspoon salt
$^1/_2$ teaspoon cracked black pepper

1 Prepare and heat barbecue. To make Tomato Relish, roughly chop tomatoes or process briefly in a food processor bowl. Combine the vinegar and sugar in medium pan. Stir over a medium heat until sugar dissolves. Bring to boil. Reduce heat and simmer 2 minutes; add tomatoes, garlic, spring onions, sun-dried tomatoes and chilli. Bring to the boil, reduce heat and simmer 35 minutes, stirring frequently.
2 Add salt and pepper and continue to cook until relish has thickened. Remove from heat and allow to cool.

3 Brush the corn with oil and cook on the hot lightly greased barbecue grill 5 minutes, each side, until corn is soft and cobs are flecked with brown in places. Using tongs, lift the corn onto the flatplate and moisten each with a square of butter. Sprinkle with salt. Serve at once with the Tomato Relish.

COOK'S FILE

Storage time: Corn is best cooked just before serving. Relish with keep several weeks in the refrigerator, stored in an airtight container.
Note: Serve relish as a spicy accompaniment to cornbread and cheese, or with barbecued sausages.

1

2

3

BARBECUED MUSHROOMS

Preparation time: 10 minutes
Total cooking time: 5 minutes
Serves 6

6 large mushrooms
50 g butter, melted
2 cloves garlic, crushed
2 tablespoons finely chopped fresh
   chives
1 tablespoon fresh thyme leaves
½ cup shredded parmesan cheese

1 Prepare and heat barbecue. Carefully peel skin from mushroom caps. Remove stalks. Combine butter and garlic in a small bowl.
2 Brush tops of mushrooms with garlic butter, place top-side down on hot barbecue flatplate and cook over the hottest part of the fire 2 minutes or until tops have browned. Turn mushrooms over. Brush upturned bases with garlic butter; cook for 2 minutes.
3 Sprinkle bases with chives and thyme, then cheese, and cook a further 3 minutes, until cheese starts to melt. Serve immediately.

COOK'S FILE
Storage time: Mushrooms are best cooked just before serving.
Hint: Mushrooms can also be cooked in a heavy-based frying pan. Lightly grease the pan with butter and cook for 2–3 minutes either side. Add fresh herbs and cheese, then place pan under hot preheated grill until cheese has melted. Any type of mushroom can be used in this recipe. Larger types such as flat or field mushrooms will take longer to cook than button or cup. Mushrooms should remain firm and chewy after cooking.

1

2

3

CHINESE VEGETABLE STIR-FRY

Preparation time: 20 minutes
Total cooking time: 6 minutes
Serves 4–6

1 medium red capsicum
100 g oyster mushrooms
425 g can baby corn
500 g Chinese cabbage
1 tablespoon olive oil
250 g fresh bean sprouts
5 spring onions, cut into 3 cm pieces
2 cloves garlic, crushed
1 tablespoon olive oil

2 teaspoons sesame oil
2 tablespoons teriyaki marinade
½ teaspoon sugar
sweet chilli sauce, to taste

1 Prepare and heat the barbecue. Cut capsicum in half, remove seeds and membrane. Cut into thin strips. Slice mushrooms in half. Cut any large baby corn in half. Cut the cabbage into thick slices, and then crosswise into squares.
2 Brush barbecue flatplate with oil. Stir-fry capsicum, mushrooms, corn, cabbage, sprouts, spring onions and garlic 4 minutes, tossing and stirring to prevent burning or sticking.

3 Pour over combined olive oil, sesame oil, teriyaki marinade and sugar, stir thoroughly to coat and cook 1 minute longer. Serve immediately. Drizzle with sweet chilli sauce.

COOK'S FILE
Storage time: Vegetables must be cooked just before serving.
Note: Teriyaki marinade is available from most supermarkets. Oyster mushrooms and Chinese cabbage are available from some greengrocers and most Asian food shops. If preferred, substitute other vegetables such as, zucchini, broccoli, cauliflower, green beans, onions or carrot. All ingredients should be about the same size to ensure even cooking.

1

2

3

Barbecued Mushrooms (top)
and Chinese Vegetable Stir-fry.

WARM PESTO PASTA SALAD

Preparation time: 20 minutes
Total cooking time: 20 minutes
Serves 4

PESTO
2 cloves garlic, crushed
1 teaspoon sea salt
¼ cup (40 g) pine nuts, toasted
2 cups (60 g) fresh basil
½ cup (50 g) grated parmesan
⅓ cup (80 ml) extra virgin olive oil

500 g orecchiette or shell pasta
2 tablespoons olive oil
150 g jar capers, drained and patted dry
2 tablespoons extra virgin olive oil
2 cloves garlic, chopped
3 tomatoes, seeded and diced
300 g thin asparagus spears, cut in
    half and blanched
2 tablespoons balsamic vinegar
200 g rocket, trimmed and cut into
    3 cm lengths
shaved parmesan,
    to garnish

1 To make the Pesto, place the garlic, sea salt and pine nuts in a food processor or blender and process until well combined. Now add the basil and parmesan and process until finely minced. With the motor still running, add the olive oil in a thin steady stream and blend until smooth.
2 Cook the pasta in a large saucepan of boiling water until al dente, then drain well.
3 Meanwhile, heat the oil in a frying pan, add the capers and fry over high heat, stirring occasionally, for 4–5 minutes, or until crisp. Remove from the pan and drain on crumpled paper towels.

4 In the same frying pan, heat the extra virgin olive oil over medium heat and add the garlic, tomato and asparagus. Cook for 1–2 minutes, or until warmed through, tossing continuously. Now stir in the balsamic vinegar.
5 Drain the pasta and transfer to a large serving bowl. Add the Pesto and toss, coating the pasta well. Cool slightly. Add the tomato mixture and rocket and season to taste with salt and cracked black pepper. Toss well and sprinkle with the capers and parmesan. Serve warm.

Fry the capers over high heat, stirring occasionally, until crisp.

Add the pesto and toss thoroughly through the pasta.

WARM CHICKPEA AND SILVERBEET SALAD

Preparation time: 30 minutes
+ overnight soaking
Total cooking time: 2 hours
Serves 4

250 g dried chickpeas
½ cup (125 ml) olive oil
1 onion, cut into thin wedges
2 tomatoes
1 teaspoon sugar
¼ teaspoon ground cinnamon
2 cloves garlic, chopped

1.5 kg silverbeet
3 tablespoons chopped fresh mint
2–3 tablespoons lemon juice
1½ tablespoons ground sumac
(see Note)

1 Place the chickpeas in a large bowl, cover with water and leave to soak overnight. Drain and place in a large saucepan. Cover with water and bring to the boil, then simmer for 1¾ hours, or until tender. Drain.
2 Heat the oil in a frying pan, add the onion and cook over low heat for 3–4 minutes, or until soft and just starting to brown. Cut the tomatoes in half, remove the seeds and dice the flesh. Add to the pan with the sugar,

cinnamon and garlic, and cook for 2–3 minutes, or until softened.
3 Wash the silverbeet and dry with paper towel. Trim the stems and finely shred the leaves. Add to the tomato mixture with the chickpeas and cook for 3–4 minutes, or until the silverbeet wilts. Add the mint, lemon juice and sumac, season, and cook for 1 minute. Serve immediately.

COOK'S FILE

Note: Sumac is available from Middle Eastern speciality shops.

Scoop the seeds out of the halved tomatoes with a teaspoon.

Add the tomato, sugar, cinnamon and garlic to the pan and cook until soft.

Add the silverbeet and chickpeas and cook until the spinach is wilted.

ROASTED FENNEL AND ORANGE SALAD

Preparation time: 30 minutes
Total cooking time: 1 hour
Serves 4

8 baby fennel bulbs
100 ml olive oil
1 teaspoon sea salt
2 oranges
1 tablespoon lemon juice
1 red onion, halved and thinly sliced
100 g Kalamata olives
2 tablespoons chopped fresh mint
1 tablespoon roughly chopped fresh
    flat-leaf parsley

1 Preheat the oven to moderately hot 200°C (400°F/Gas 6). Trim and reserve the fennel fronds. Remove the stalks and cut a slice off the base of each fennel about 5 mm thick. Slice each fennel into 6 wedges. Place in a baking dish and drizzle with ¼ cup (60 ml) of the oil. Add the salt and plenty of pepper. Bake for 40–60 minutes, or until the fennel is tender and slightly caramelised. Cool.

2 Cut a slice off the top and bottom of each orange. Using a small sharp knife, slice off the skin and pith, following the curves of the orange. Remove as much pith as possible. Slice down the side of a segment between the flesh and the membrane. Repeat with the other side and lift the segment out. Do this over a bowl to catch the segments and juices. Repeat with all the segments. Squeeze any juice from the membrane. Drain and reserve the juice.

3 Whisk the remaining olive oil into the orange juice and the lemon juice until emulsified. Season well. Combine the orange segments, onion and olives in a bowl, pour on half the dressing and add half the mint. Mix well. Transfer to a serving dish. Top with the roasted fennel, drizzle with the remaining dressing, and scatter with the parsley and the remaining mint. Roughly chop the reserved fronds and scatter over the salad.

Use a sharp knife to slice each of the baby fennels into wedges.

Bake the fennel until tender and slightly caramelised.

Remove the orange skin and pith with a small sharp knife.

Cut the orange between the flesh and the membrane to remove the segments.

GREEK SALAD

Preparation time: 20 minutes
Total cooking time: Nil
Serves 4

4 tomatoes, cut into wedges
1 telegraph cucumber, peeled, halved, seeded and cut into small cubes
2 green capsicums, seeded, halved lengthways and cut into strips
1 red onion, finely sliced
16 Kalamata olives
250 g good-quality firm feta, cut into cubes
3 tablespoons fresh flat-leaf parsley leaves
12 whole fresh mint leaves
½ cup (125 ml) good-quality olive oil
2 tablespoons lemon juice
1 clove garlic, crushed

1 Place the tomato, cucumber, capsicum, onion, olives, feta and half the parsley and mint leaves in a large salad bowl, and gently mix together.
2 Place the oil, juice and garlic in a screw-top jar, season and shake until combined. Pour the dressing over the salad and lightly toss. Garnish with the remaining parsley and mint.

Peel, halve and seed the cucumber, then cut into small cubes.

Cut the good-quality firm feta into even-sized cubes.

Gently mix the salad ingredients together, without breaking up the feta.

121

LENTIL SALAD

Preparation time: 15 minutes
+ 30 minutes standing
Total cooking time: 30 minutes
Serves 4–6

1/2 brown onion
2 cloves
1 1/2 cups (300 g) puy lentils (see Note)
1 strip lemon rind
2 cloves garlic, peeled
1 fresh bay leaf
2 teaspoons ground cumin

2 tablespoons red wine vinegar
1/4 cup (60 ml) olive oil
1 tablespoon lemon juice
2 tablespoon fresh mint leaves,
   finely chopped
3 spring onions, finely chopped

1 Stud the onion with the cloves and place in a saucepan with the lentils, rind, garlic, bay leaf, 1 teaspoon cumin and 3 1/2 cups (875 ml) water. Bring to the boil and cook over medium heat for 25–30 minutes, or until the water has been absorbed. Discard the onion, rind and the bay leaf. Reserve the garlic and finely chop.

2 Whisk together the vinegar, oil, juice, garlic and remaining cumin. Stir through the lentils with the mint and spring onion. Season well. Leave for 30 minutes to let the flavours absorb. Serve at room temperature.

COOK'S FILE
Note: Puy lentils are small, green lentils from France. They are available dried from gourmet food stores.

Stud the brown onion half with the cloves.

Cook the lentils, then discard the onion, lemon rind and bay leaf.

Whisk together the vinegar, oil, lemon juice, garlic and cumin.

TOMATO AND BOCCONCINI SALAD

Preparation time: 10 minutes
Total cooking time: Nil
Serves 4

3 large vine-ripened tomatoes
250 g bocconcini (see Note)
12 fresh basil leaves
¼ cup (60 ml) extra virgin olive oil
4 basil leaves, roughly torn, extra, optional

1 Slice the tomatoes into 1 cm slices, making twelve slices altogether. Slice the bocconcini into twenty-four 1 cm slices.
2 Arrange the tomato slices on a serving plate, alternating them with two slices of bocconcini. Place the basil leaves between the slices of bocconcini.
3 Drizzle with the oil, sprinkle with the basil, if desired, and season well with salt and ground black pepper.

COOK'S FILE
Note: This popular summer salad is most successful with very fresh buffalo mozzarella if you can find it. We've used bocconcini in this recipe as it can be difficult to find very fresh mozzarella.

Slice the bocconcini into twenty-four 1 cm thick slices.

Arrange the tomato slices on a serving plate, alternating with the bocconcini.

TABBOULEH

Preparation time: 20 minutes
+ 1 hour 30 minutes soaking
+ 30 minutes drying
Total cooking time: Nil
Serves 6

¾ cup (130 g) cracked wheat (burghul)
3 ripe tomatoes (300 g)
1 telegraph cucumber
4 spring onions, sliced
4 cups (120 g) chopped fresh
  flat-leaf parsley
¼ cup (10 g) fresh mint, chopped

DRESSING
⅓ cup (80 ml) lemon juice
¼ cup (60 ml) olive oil
1 tablespoon extra virgin olive oil

1 Place the cracked wheat (burghul) in a bowl, cover with 2 cups (500 ml) water and leave for 1 hour 30 minutes.
2 Cut the tomatoes in half, squeeze gently to remove any excess seeds and cut into 1 cm cubes. Cut the cucumber in half lengthways, remove the seeds with a teaspoon and cut the flesh into 1 cm cubes.
3 To make the dressing, whisk the lemon juice and 1½ teaspoons salt in a bowl until well combined. Season well with freshly ground black pepper and slowly whisk in the olive oil and extra virgin olive oil.
4 Drain the wheat and squeeze out any excess water. Spread the burghul on a clean tea towel or paper towels and leave to dry for 30 minutes. Place the burghul in a large salad bowl, add the tomato, cucumber, spring onion and herbs, and toss to combine. Pour the dressing over the salad and toss until evenly coated. Delicious served with bread.

Whisk the olive oil and extra virgin olive oil into the lemon juice.

Drain the wheat and squeeze out any excess water.

Toss the salad ingredients together before adding the dressing.

WILD AND BROWN RICE SALAD

Preparation time: 10 minutes
Total cooking time: 1 hour
15 minutes
Serves 6–8

1 cup brown rice
½ cup wild rice
1 medium red onion
1 small red capsicum
2 sticks celery
2 tablespoons chopped

fresh parsley
⅓ cup chopped pecans

DRESSING
¼ cup orange juice
¼ cup lemon juice
1 teaspoon finely grated orange rind
1 teaspoon finely grated lemon rind
⅓ cup olive oil

1 Cook brown rice in a pan of boiling water 25–30 minutes until just tender. Drain well and cool completely. Boil wild rice 30–40 minutes; drain well and cool. Chop onion and capsicum finely. Cut celery into thin slices. Combine in bowl with parsley and cooked rices. Place pecans in a dry frying pan and stir over medium heat 2–3 minutes until lightly toasted. Transfer to plate to cool.

2 To make Dressing, place juices, rinds and oil in a small screwtop jar; shake well to combine.

3 Pour dressing over salad and fold through. Add pecans and gently mix through. Serve with bread, if desired.

COOK'S FILE

Storage time: Salad can be assembled up to 4 hours in advance.

1

2

3

SALAD NIÇOISE

Preparation time: 30 minutes
Total cooking time: 15 minutes
Serves 4

3 eggs
2 vine-ripened tomatoes
175 g baby green beans, trimmed
½ cup (125 ml) olive oil
2 tablespoons white wine vinegar
1 large clove garlic, halved
325 g iceberg lettuce heart, cut
    into 8 wedges
1 small red capsicum, seeded and
    thinly sliced
1 celery stick, cut into 5 cm thin strips
1 Lebanese cucumber, cut into thin
    5 cm lengths

¼ large red onion, thinly sliced
2 x 185 g cans tuna, drained,
    broken into chunks
12 Kalamata olives
45 g can anchovy fillets, drained
2 teaspoons baby capers
12 small fresh basil leaves

1 Place the eggs in a saucepan of
cold water. Bring slowly to the boil,
then reduce the heat and simmer for
10 minutes. Stir during the first few
minutes to centre the yolks. Cool the
eggs under cold water, then peel and
cut into quarters. Meanwhile, score
a cross in the base of each tomato.
Place the tomatoes in a bowl of
boiling water for 1 minute, then
plunge into cold water and peel
the skin away from the cross.
Cut into eighths.

2 Cook the beans in a saucepan of
boiling water for 2 minutes, then
refresh quickly under cold water and
drain. Place the oil and vinegar in a
jar and shake to combine.
3 Rub the garlic halves over the base
and sides of a large salad serving
platter. Arrange the lettuce wedges
evenly over the base. Layer the
tomato, capsicum, celery, cucumber,
beans and egg quarters over the
lettuce. Scatter with the onion and
tuna. Arrange the olives, anchovies,
capers and basil leaves over the top,
pour the dressing over the salad and
serve immediately.

*Using a sharp knife, cut the celery stick
into long, thin strips.*

*Cut the peeled tomatoes into quarters,
and again into eighths.*

*Layer the tomato, capsicum, celery,
cucumber, beans and egg over the lettuce.*

126

SPINACH SALAD

Preparation time: 20 minutes
Total cooking time: 20 minutes
Serves 2–4

3 slices white bread, crusts removed
150 g (5 oz) English spinach leaves
2–3 tablespoons pine nuts
3 rashers bacon, chopped
8 button mushrooms, finely sliced
¼ cup (7 g/ ¼ oz) basil leaves,
    shredded
1–2 cloves garlic, crushed
2–3 tablespoons olive oil

balsamic vinegar or freshly squeezed
    lemon juice, to taste

1 Preheat the oven to moderately hot 190°C (375°F/Gas 5). Cut the bread into small cubes, spread on a baking tray and bake for 10 minutes, or until the bread cubes are golden.
2 Gently rinse the spinach leaves under cold water. Bundle them in a clean tea towel and shake gently to remove the water. Tear into pieces and place in a large serving bowl. Put the pine nuts in a non-stick frying pan and stir gently over low heat until golden brown. Remove and cool

slightly. Add the bacon to the pan and cook for 5–6 minutes, or until crispy. Remove and drain on paper towels.
3 Add the pine nuts, bacon, bread cubes, mushrooms and basil to the spinach leaves. Whisk the garlic and oil together and pour over the salad, mixing gently. Drizzle with the vinegar or lemon juice. Sprinkle with salt and freshly ground pepper, and serve immediately.

Cut the bread into small cubes and spread on a baking tray.

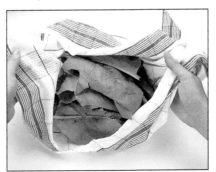

Bundle the spinach leaves in a tea towel and shake to remove the excess water.

Pour the combined garlic and oil over the salad, mixing gently.

127

CURLY ENDIVE SALAD WITH CRISP PROSCIUTTO AND GARLIC CROUTONS

Preparation time: 20 minutes
Total cooking time: Nil
Serves 4–6

1 large bunch curly endive
½ red oak leaf lettuce
2 red onions
4 slices white or
    brown bread
2 large cloves garlic, crushed
50 g butter, softened
35 g feta cheese, mashed
4–6 thin slices prosciutto ham
1 large avocado

DRESSING
2 tablespoons olive oil
¼ cup sugar
¼ cup spicy tomato sauce
1 tablespoon soy sauce
⅓ cup red wine vinegar

1 Rinse endive and oak leaf lettuce in cold water. Shake lightly in tea-towel to absorb excess water. Tear endive and lettuce into pieces. Peel and slice onions; separate into rings. Combine endive, lettuce and onions in salad bowl.
2 Toast bread one side only. Mash garlic, butter and feta cheese into a paste, spread over the untoasted side of the bread. Remove crusts; toast buttered side of bread until crisp and golden on the surface. Cut each slice into 1 cm cubes.
3 Place prosciutto under very hot grill for a few seconds until crisp. Remove and cut into 5 cm pieces. Set aside. Cut avocado into thin wedges.
4 To make Dressing, whisk oil, sugar, tomato sauce, soy sauce and vinegar together in bowl. Add prosciutto and avocado to the salad and pour over half the dressing. Arrange croûtons on top and serve remaining dressing in a jug.

COOK'S FILE
Storage time: Dressing can be made 1 day in advance, but salad must be made and dressed just before serving.

TRI-COLOUR PASTA SALAD

Preparation time: 20 minutes
Total cooking time: 10 minutes
Serves 6

2 tablespoons olive oil
2 tablespoons white wine vinegar
1 small garlic clove, halved
375 g tri-colour pasta spirals
1 tablespoon olive oil, extra
¼ cup sun-dried tomatoes in oil, drained

½ cup black pitted olives
100 g parmesan cheese
1 cup quartered artichoke hearts
½ cup shredded fresh basil leaves

1 Combine olive oil, vinegar and garlic in a small screwtop jar. Shake well to mix and allow to stand 1 hour. Cook pasta in a large pan of boiling water until just tender. Drain and toss with extra olive oil while still hot. Allow to cool completely.
2 Cut sun-dried tomatoes into fine strips and cut olives in half. Cut parmesan into paper-thin slices.
3 Place pasta, tomatoes, olives, cheese, artichokes and basil in a large serving bowl. Pour dressing over, remove garlic pieces, and toss to combine. Serve immediately.

COOK'S FILE

Storage time: Salad can be assembled up to 4 hours in advance. Refrigerate until required; allow to come to room temperature. Add cheese and basil just before serving.
Hint: Serve this salad with barbecued steak or roast chicken.

1

2

3

ROSEMARY SAUTÉED POTATOES

Preparation time: 10 minutes
Total cooking time: 25 minutes
Serves 6

4–5 large potatoes (about 1.5 kg)
⅓ cup olive oil
1 tablespoon chopped fresh rosemary
1 clove garlic, crushed
salt and black pepper, to taste

1 Peel potatoes and cut into 2 cm cubes. Rinse the potatoes in cold water, drain well and dry thoroughly on a clean tea-towel.

2 Heat oil in large heavy-based frying pan. Add potatoes and cook slowly, shaking pan occasionally, 20 minutes or until tender. Turn potatoes often to prevent sticking. Partially cover pan halfway through cooking. The steam will help cook the potato.

3 Add the rosemary and garlic, with salt and pepper to taste, in the last few minutes of cooking. Increase the heat to crisp the potatoes, if required.

COOK'S FILE

Storage time: Potatoes can be cooked ahead of time and reheated in a heavy-based pan moistened with olive oil, over the barbecue.

Note: Potatoes can be cooked on a large barbecue flatplate, provided the heat is not too intense. If the potatoes cook too quickly, the surface will burn without cooking through to the centre. Parboil cubed potatoes 2–5 minutes before barbecuing, if desired.

1

2

3

STUFFED CAPSICUM

Preparation time: 20 minutes
Total cooking time: 40 minutes
Serves 4

⅓ cup (80 ml) olive oil
⅔ cup (125 g) couscous
15 g butter
4 large red or yellow capsicums
3 tablespoons pine nuts
1 onion, finely chopped
2 teaspoons ground cumin
1 teaspoon ground coriander
75 g raisins
3 tablespoons chopped fresh mint
2 tablespoons chopped fresh
    coriander leaves

YOGHURT DRESSING
1 cup (250 g) Greek-style plain
    yoghurt
2 tablespoons chopped fresh mint

1 Place 1 cup (250 ml) water in a saucepan and bring to the boil. Add 1 tablespoon of the olive oil, a pinch of salt and the couscous. Remove from the heat and leave for 2 minutes, or until the couscous is tender and has absorbed all the liquid. Stir in the butter with a fork and cook over low heat for 3 minutes.

2 Preheat the oven to moderately hot 190°C (375°F/Gas 5). Lightly grease a baking tray. Slice the tops off the capsicums and remove the seeds and membrane, reserving the tops. Plunge the capsicums into a saucepan of boiling water for 2 minutes, then drain on paper towels.

3 Heat a frying pan over high heat. Add the pine nuts and dry-fry for 2–3 minutes, or until golden brown. Remove the pine nuts from the pan. Heat 1 tablespoon of the olive oil in the pan, add the onion and cook over medium heat for 5 minutes, or until softened. Add the cumin and coriander, and cook for 1 minute. Remove from the heat and stir into the couscous with the pine nuts, raisins and herbs, and season well.

4 Fill each capsicum with some of the couscous stuffing and place on the tray. Drizzle the remaining olive oil over the capsicums and replace the lids. Bake for 20–25 minutes, or until tender. Meanwhile, combine the yoghurt and mint, and place in a serving dish. Serve the capsicums with the dressing and a salad.

Add the butter to the couscous and cook for 3 minutes.

Spoon the couscous mixture into the capsicum shells.

131

GREEN BEANS WITH TOMATO AND OLIVE OIL

Preparation time: 10 minutes
Total cooking time: 25 minutes
Serves 4

¹/₃ cup (80 ml) olive oil
1 large onion, chopped
3 cloves garlic, finely chopped
400 g can diced tomatoes

¹/₂ teaspoon sugar
750 g green beans, trimmed
3 tablespoons chopped fresh
    flat-leaf parsley

1 Heat the olive oil in a large frying pan, add the onion and cook over medium heat for 4–5 minutes, or until softened. Add the garlic and cook for a further 30 seconds.
2 Add ¹/₂ cup (125 ml) water, the tomato and sugar and season, to taste. Bring to the boil, then reduce the heat and simmer for 10 minutes, or until reduced slightly.
3 Add the beans and parsley and simmer for a further 10 minutes, or until the beans are tender and the tomato mixture is pulpy. Season with salt and black pepper, and serve immediately as a side dish.

Using a sharp knife, finely chop the garlic cloves.

Cook the chopped onion in the olive oil until softened.

Simmer the tomato mixture until reduced slightly.

132

LEBANESE TOASTED BREAD SALAD

Preparation time: 15 minutes
Total cooking time: 10 minutes
Serves 6

2 pitta bread rounds
(17 cm diameter)
6 cos lettuce leaves, shredded
1 large Lebanese cucumber, cubed
4 tomatoes, cut into 1 cm cubes
8 spring onions, chopped
4 tablespoons finely chopped fresh
   flat-leaf parsley

1 tablespoon finely chopped fresh
   mint
2 tablespoons finely chopped fresh
   coriander

DRESSING

2 cloves garlic, crushed
100 ml extra virgin olive oil
100 ml lemon juice

1 Preheat the oven to moderate 180°C (350°F/Gas 4). Split the bread in half through the centre and bake on a baking tray for 8–10 minutes, or until golden and crisp, turning halfway through. Break the bread into pieces.

2 To make the dressing, whisk all the ingredients together in a bowl until combined.

3 Place the bread and remaining salad ingredients in a serving bowl and toss to combine. Pour on the dressing and toss well. Season to taste with salt and freshly ground black pepper. Serve immediately.

COOK'S FILE

Note: This is a popular Middle Eastern peasant salad which can be served either as an appetiser or to accompany a light meal.

Split the pitta bread rounds in two through the centre.

Once the bread is golden and crisp, break it into small pieces.

Place the bread pieces and salad ingredients in a bowl and toss well.

ROASTED BALSAMIC ONIONS

Preparation time: 15 minutes
+ overnight refrigeration
Total cooking time: 1 hour 30 minutes
Serves 8 (as part of an antipasto platter)

1 kg (2 lb) pickling onions, unpeeled (see Note)
¾ cup (185 ml/6 fl oz) balsamic vinegar
2 tablespoons soft brown sugar
¾ cup (185 ml/6 fl oz) olive oil

1 Preheat the oven to warm 160°C (315°F/Gas 2–3). Place the unpeeled onions in a baking dish and roast for 1½ hours. Leave until cool enough to handle. Trim the stems from the onions and peel away the skin (the outer part of the root should come away but the onions will remain intact). Rinse a 1-litre wide-necked jar with boiling water and dry in a warm oven (do not dry with a tea towel). Add the onions to the jar.
2 Combine the vinegar and sugar in a small screw-top jar and stir to dissolve the sugar. Add the oil, seal the jar and shake vigorously until combined—the mixture will be paler and may separate on standing.
3 Pour the vinegar mixture over the onions, seal, and turn upside down

to coat. Marinate overnight in the refrigerator, turning occasionally. Return to room temperature and shake to combine the dressing before serving.

COOK'S FILE

Note: Pickling onions are very small, usually packed in 1 kg (2 lb) bags. The ideal size is around 35 g (1¼ oz) each. The sizes in the bag will probably range from 20 g (¾ oz) up to 40 g (1¼ oz). The cooking time given is suitable for this range and there is no need to cook the larger ones for any longer. The marinating time given is a minimum time and the onions may be marinated for up to 3 days in the refrigerator. The marinade may separate after a few hours, which is fine —simply stir occasionally.

When cool, trim the stems from the onions and peel away the skin.

Add the oil to the vinegar and sugar and shake vigorously to combine.

Pour the vinegar mixture over the onions; turn the jar to coat well.

ROAST BEETROOT AND ONION WEDGE SALAD

Preparation time: 30 minutes
Total cooking time: 1 hour
30 minutes
Serves 4–6

4 medium beetroots
3 red onions
⅓ cup (80 ml/2¾ fl oz) oil
20 g (¾ oz) butter
1 teaspoon ground cumin
1 teaspoon soft brown sugar
2 tablespoons orange juice
2 tablespoons orange zest
chopped chives, to garnish

SOUR CREAM DRESSING
150 g (5 oz) sour cream
2 tablespoons chopped chives
1 tablespoon chopped thyme
1 teaspoon lemon juice

1 Preheat the oven to moderate 180°C (350°F/Gas 4). Trim the leafy tops from the beetroot, leaving a 4 cm (1½ inch) stalk, and wash thoroughly. Keep the beetroot whole to avoid bleeding during baking. Cut each onion into 6 large wedges, leaving the bases intact as much as possible so the wedges hold together. Put the oil in a large baking dish and add the beetroot and onion wedges. Bake for 1 hour 15 minutes. Remove the beetroot and onion onto separate plates and set aside to cool slightly. Peel and discard the skins from the beetroot. Trim the tops and tails off the beetroot to neaten, and cut into large wedges.
2 Heat the butter in a frying pan, add the cumin and brown sugar, and cook for 1 minute. Add the orange juice

and simmer for 5 minutes, or until the juice has reduced slightly. Add the baked beetroot wedges and orange zest, and stir gently over low heat for 2 minutes.
3 To make the dressing, combine the sour cream, chopped chives, thyme

and lemon juice. Arrange the cooked beetroot and onion wedges on a large serving plate and serve with the dressing. Sprinkle with the chopped chives to garnish.

Trim the leafy tops from the beetroots, leaving a short stalk.

Cut onions into wedges, leaving as much of the base intact as possible.

Add the beetroot wedges and orange zest to the pan.

135

VINAIGRETTES

Vinaigrettes are classic salad dressings made from vinegar and oil.
While the simplest vinaigrette may consist of just balsamic vinegar and extra virgin
olive oil, these easy variations use herbs and fruit for added flavour.

BASIC VINAIGRETTE
Put 2 tablespoons white wine vinegar, ⅓ cup (80 ml/2¾
fl oz) light olive oil and 1 teaspoon Dijon mustard in a small
screw-top jar. Season with salt and cracked black pepper
and shake until well blended. Will keep, covered, in the
fridge for up to 2 days. Makes ⅓ cup (80 ml/2¾ fl oz).

LEMON THYME AND LIME VINAIGRETTE
Put ⅔ cup (170 ml/5½ fl oz) light olive oil, ⅓ cup (80
ml/2¾ fl oz) lime juice, 2 tablespoons lemon thyme leaves
and 1 teaspoon honey in a screw-top jar. Season with salt
and pepper and shake well. Will keep, covered, in the
refrigerator for up to 2 days. Makes 1 cup (250 ml/8 fl oz).

STRAWBERRY VINAIGRETTE
Place ⅓ cup (80 ml/2¾ fl oz) light olive oil, 2 tablespoons
strawberry vinegar, ½ teaspoon Dijon mustard and
½ teaspoon sugar in a screw-top jar. Season with salt
and pepper and shake well. Will keep, covered, in the
fridge for up to 2 days. Makes ½ cup (125 ml/4 fl oz).

BALSAMIC AND BASIL VINAIGRETTE
Put 2 tablespoons balsamic vinegar, ⅓ cup (80 ml/2¾ fl
oz) extra virgin olive oil, 1 crushed clove garlic and
2 tablespoons shredded basil in a screw-top jar. Season,
to taste, and shake until mixed. Refrigerate, covered, for
up to 2 days. Makes ⅓ cup (80 ml/2¾ fl oz).

LEMON GRASS AND LIME VINAIGRETTE

Mix ½ cup (125 ml/4 fl oz) oil, ½ cup (125 ml/ 4 fl oz) lime juice, 3 teaspoons sesame oil, 2 tablespoons finely sliced lemon grass, 1 crushed clove garlic and 2 teaspoons soft brown sugar in a screw-top jar. Season with salt and pepper and shake well to combine. Will keep, covered, in the refrigerator for up to 2 days. Makes 1¼ cups (315 ml/10 fl oz).

PISTACHIO AND TARRAGON VINAIGRETTE

Put ⅓ cup (80 ml/2¾ fl oz) light olive oil, 1 tablespoon pistachio oil, 2 tablespoons white wine vinegar, 1 tablespoon chopped pistachios, 1 tablespoon chopped tarragon and ¼ teaspoon sugar in a screw-top jar. Season with salt and pepper and shake well to combine. Will keep, covered, in the refrigerator for up to 2 days. Makes ⅓ cup (80 ml/2¾ fl oz).

ORANGE AND MUSTARD SEED VINAIGRETTE

Mix ⅓ cup (80 ml/2¾ fl oz) orange juice, 2 tablespoons vinegar, ⅓ cup (80 ml/2¾ fl oz) light olive oil, ½ teaspoon finely grated orange rind and 2 teaspoons wholegrain mustard in a screw-top jar. Season with salt and pepper and shake well. Will keep, covered, in the fridge for up to 2 days. Makes ⅔ cup (160 ml/5½ fl oz).

RASPBERRY VINAIGRETTE

Place ⅓ cup (80 ml/2¾ fl oz) hazelnut oil, 2 tablespoons raspberry vinegar, 5 finely chopped raspberries and ½ teaspoon sugar in a small screw-top jar. Season with salt and white pepper and shake to blend. Will keep, covered, in the fridge for up to 2 days. Makes ⅓ cup (80 ml/2¾ fl oz).

Top, from left: Basic Vinaigrette; Strawberry; Lemon Grass and Lime; Orange and Mustard Seed. Bottom, from left: Lemon Thyme and Lime; Balsamic and Basil; Pistachio and Tarragon; Raspberry.

MAYONNAISE AND DRESSINGS

Most of us buy mayonnaise in the supermarket, taking a chance as to whether
it's rich and creamy or, as is often the case, gluey and oversweet. Try making your own—
it's actually very easy and you'll get a good-quality result every time.

MAYONNAISE

Whisk together 2 egg yolks, 1 teaspoon Dijon mustard and
1 tablespoon lemon juice for 30 seconds, or until light and
creamy. Add ¾ cup (185 ml/6 fl oz) olive oil, about a
teaspoon at a time, whisking continuously. You can add
the oil more quickly as the mayonnaise thickens. Season,
to taste, with salt and white pepper.

Alternatively, place the egg yolks, mustard and lemon
juice in a food processor and mix for 10 seconds. With the
motor running, add the oil in a slow, thin stream. Season,
to taste. Makes about 1 cup (250 ml/8 fl oz)

THOUSAND ISLAND DRESSING

Mix together 1½ cups (375 ml/12 fl oz) mayonnaise,
1 tablespoon sweet chilli sauce, 1–2 tablespoons tomato
sauce, ¼ red capsicum and ¼ green capsicum, finely
chopped, 1 tablespoon chopped chives and ½ teaspoon
sweet paprika. Stir well and season. Cover and refrigerate
for up to 3 days. Thousand Island Dressing is traditionally
served on lettuce leaves. Makes 1⅔ cups (410 ml/13 fl oz).

GREEN GODDESS DRESSING

Mix together 1½ cups (375 ml/12 fl oz) mayonnaise,
4 mashed anchovy fillets, 4 finely chopped spring
onions, 1 crushed clove garlic, ¼ cup (7 g/¼ oz) chopped
flat-leaf parsley, ¼ cup (15 g/½ oz) finely chopped
chives and 1 teaspoon tarragon vinegar. Serve as a
salad dressing or with seafood. Makes about 1⅔ cups
(410 ml/13 fl oz).

AIOLI (GARLIC MAYONNAISE)

Mix together 1 cup (250 ml/8 fl oz) mayonnaise with
3 crushed cloves of garlic. Season, to taste, with salt and
pepper. Makes about 1 cup (250 ml/8 fl oz).

COCKTAIL SAUCE

Mix together 1 cup (250 ml/8 fl oz) mayonnaise, 3
tablespoons tomato sauce, 2 teaspoons Worcestershire sauce,
½ teaspoon lemon juice and 1 drop of Tabasco sauce.
Season with salt and pepper. Keep, covered, in the fridge
for up to 2 days. Makes about 1¼ cups (315 ml/10 fl oz).

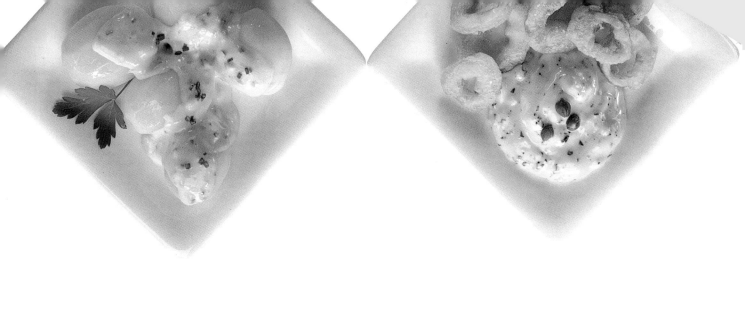

BLUE CHEESE DRESSING

Mix together ½ cup (125 ml/4 fl oz) mayonnaise, ¼ cup (60 ml/2 fl oz) thick cream, 1 teaspoon white wine vinegar and 1 tablespoon finely chopped chives. Crumble 50 g (1¾ oz) blue cheese into the mixture and gently stir through. Season with salt and white pepper. Can be kept refrigerated, covered, for up to 2 days. Serve over asparagus, boiled new potatoes, jacket potatoes or with a green salad. Makes about 1 cup (250 ml/8 fl oz).

CAESAR SALAD DRESSING

Cook an egg in boiling water for 1 minute. Break the egg into a small bowl and add 2 tablespoons white wine or tarragon vinegar, 2 teaspoons Dijon mustard, 2 chopped anchovy fillets and 1 crushed clove garlic. Mix together with a small wire whisk. Add ½ cup (125 ml/4 fl oz) oil in a thin stream, whisking continuously until the mixture is smooth and creamy. Keep, covered, in the fridge for up to 2 days. Serve on Caesar salad (cos lettuce, bacon, croutons and parmesan). Makes about ¾ cup (185 ml/6 fl oz).

TARTARE SAUCE

Mix together 1½ cups (375 ml/12 fl oz) mayonnaise, 1 tablespoon finely chopped onion, 1 teaspoon lemon juice, 1 tablespoon chopped gherkins, 1 teaspoon chopped capers, ¼ teaspoon Dijon mustard and 1 tablespoon finely chopped parsley. Mix well and season with salt and pepper. Top with a few capers to serve. Makes about 1⅔ cups (410 ml/13 fl oz).

Top, from left: Mayonnaise; Thousand Island; Blue Cheese; Tartare Sauce. Bottom, from left: Aioli; Green Goddess; Caesar Salad; Cocktail Sauce.

BREADS

GARLIC BREAD

Cut a French loaf into thick diagonal slices three-quarters of the way through. Combine 125 g softened butter, 2–3 cloves crushed garlic, 1 tablespoon finely chopped parsley and pepper, to taste, in small bowl. Beat until smooth. Spread mixture between each slice of bread. Wrap bread in foil and place on baking tray. Bake in moderate 180°C oven for 10–15 minutes or until butter has melted and bread is hot. Alternatively, place bread on hot barbecue grill or flatplate, turning occasionally to ensure even cooking.

BACON AND CHEESE BREAD

Combine ½ cup grated cheddar cheese, 2 tablespoons grated parmesan cheese, 1 finely sliced spring onion, 2 finely chopped bacon rashers and pepper, to taste, in a small bowl. Across the top of a Vienna loaf, at 2 cm intervals, cut diagonal slits 1 cm deep in one direction. Make similar slits in the opposite direction crossing over the first cuts, forming a diamond pattern. Place bread on a foil-lined baking tray. Sprinkle cheese and bacon mixture over the top. Bake loaf in a preheated 180°C oven 10–15 minutes or until cheese has melted and bacon is crisp. Cut into slices and serve hot with butter.

PESTO ROLLS

Combine ¼ cup toasted pine nuts, 2–3 tablespoons freshly grated parmesan cheese, 1–2 cloves peeled garlic, 2 tablespoons olive oil, 50 g chopped butter, 3–4 teaspoons lemon juice, 1 cup fresh basil leaves, salt and pepper, to taste, in food processor bowl. Process 20–30 seconds or until smooth. (Add a little more butter or oil if pesto is dry.) Cut 6 small dinner rolls in half vertically. Spread each half with mixture. Toast rolls under preheated grill 5–10 minutes or until heated through. Serve with shavings of parmesan cheese. Alternatively, place roll halves together; wrap in foil. Place on hot barbecue grill, turning occasionally.

TOMATO AND OLIVE BREAD

Cut a French bread stick into 2 cm thick slices using a sharp serrated knife. Spread each slice with a small amount of green or black olive paste. Thinly slice 2 tomatoes. Place 1 or 2 slices of tomato on each slice of bread. Top with thinly sliced mozzarella or bocconcini (fresh mozzarella). Sprinkle with pepper and 2–3 tablespoons finely shredded basil leaves. Place on foil-lined baking tray. Bake in preheated moderate 180°C oven 10–15 minutes or until cheese has melted and bread has heated through. Serve warm.

From top left: Bacon and Cheese Bread, Garlic Bread, Tomato and Olive Bread, Pesto Rolls.

ROASTED RED CAPSICUM BUNS

Preparation time: 40 minutes
+ 1 hour 40 minutes rising
Total cooking time: 1 hour
Makes 8 buns

2 red capsicums, cut into large flat pieces
7 g (¼ oz) dried yeast
2 teaspoons sugar
4 cups (500 g/1 lb) plain flour
1 teaspoon salt
1 tablespoon olive oil
1 egg, lightly beaten

1 Place the capsicum skin-side-up under a hot grill, until the skins blacken. Cool in a plastic bag, then peel away the skin and cut the capsicum into cubes.
2 Combine the dried yeast, sugar and ½ cup (125 ml/4 fl oz) of warm water in a bowl and leave in a warm place for 10 minutes, or until frothy.
3 Sift the flour and salt into a bowl, make a well in the centre and pour in the oil, the frothy yeast and 1¼ cups (315 ml/10 fl oz) of warm water. Mix to a soft dough, gather into a ball and knead on a floured surface until smooth. Add a little extra flour if needed. Place in a lightly oiled bowl, cover loosely with greased plastic

wrap and leave in a warm place for 1 hour, or until doubled.
4 Punch down the dough, turn out onto a floured surface and knead for 10 minutes, adding the capsicum half way through. Divide the dough into eight and form into rounds. Lay apart on a greased baking tray. Cover with a damp tea towel and leave for 30 minutes, or until well risen. Preheat the oven to moderate 180°C (350°F/ Gas 4). Brush the buns with beaten egg. Bake for 40–45 minutes, or until the base sounds hollow when tapped.

Sift the flour and salt together into a large bowl.

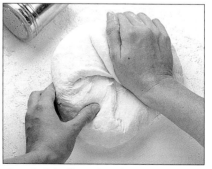

On a lightly floured surface, knead the dough until smooth.

On a well-floured surface, knead in the capsicum.

SAVOURY SCROLL

Preparation time: 35 minutes
Total cooking time: 35 minutes
Serves 6

1 cup (125 g/4 oz) grated cheddar
¼ cup (25 g/¾ oz) grated parmesan
1 onion, chopped
1 red capsicum, chopped
100 g (3¼ oz) pancetta, chopped
¼ cup (15 g/½ oz) chopped parsley
3 cups (375 g/12 oz) self-raising flour
1 teaspoon salt
60 g (2 oz) butter, cubed
1¼ cups (315 ml/10 fl oz) buttermilk
2 tablespoons olive oil

1 Grease 1 baking tray. Preheat the oven to moderately hot 200°C (400°F/Gas 6). To make the filling, combine the cheddar, parmesan, onion, capsicum, pancetta and parsley. Season well with salt and pepper.

2 Sift the flour and salt into a large bowl. Add the butter and rub in with your fingertips until the mixture is crumbly. Make a well in the centre and pour in the buttermilk; mix to a soft dough and gather into a ball. Turn out onto a lightly floured surface and knead until smooth and elastic.

3 Roll out to a 50 x 25 cm (20 x 10 inch) rectangle. Sprinkle the filling over the top, leaving a 2 cm (¾ inch) border and press the filling down slightly. Roll up lengthways, enclosing the filling. Bring the ends together to form a ring and brush the ends with some water. Press to seal.

4 Place on the prepared tray, snip the outside edge of the scroll with scissors at regular intervals, so the filling is exposed. Bake for 15 minutes, reduce the temperature to moderate 180°C (350°F/Gas 4) and bake for a further 20 minutes, or until golden brown. Brush with the olive oil.

Cube the onion and capsicum and chop the pancetta into small pieces.

Using your fingertips, rub the butter into the flour.

Tightly roll up the filled dough lengthways into a log shape.

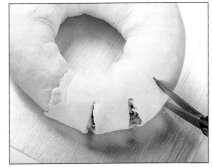

Using sharp scissors, snip the out-side edge of the scroll at intervals.

PUMPKIN DAMPER

Preparation time: 25 minutes
Total cooking time: 25 minutes
Serves 8

1 cup (125 g/4 oz) self-raising flour
1½ cups (225 g/7¼ oz) wholemeal
   self-raising flour
1 teaspoon baking powder
1 teaspoon salt
3 tablespoons grated parmesan
1 egg, lightly beaten
2 teaspoons tomato paste

1 cup (250 g/8 oz) mashed pumpkin,
   well-drained (see Note)
3 tablespoons chopped fresh basil
30 g (1 oz) butter, melted
3 tablespoons milk
2 tablespoons pumpkin
   seeds (pepitas)

1 Preheat the oven to hot 210°C
(415°F/Gas 6–7). Grease a baking
tray. Sift the flours, baking powder
and salt together into a bowl and
return the husks. Add the parmesan
and mix in the egg, tomato paste,
pumpkin, basil, butter and milk.
Mix to a soft dough.

2 Turn out onto a floured surface and
knead until smooth. Flatten out to a
circle 20 cm (8 inches) in diameter.
3 Place on the baking tray. Using a
sharp knife, mark into 8 portions.
Brush with water and sprinkle with
the pepitas. Bake for 25 minutes, or
until cooked through.

COOK'S FILE
Note: You will need 400 g (13 oz) of
unpeeled raw pumpkin.

*Mix together the mashed pumpkin, egg,
tomato paste, basil, butter and milk.*

*Cut through the mixture with a flat-
bladed knife until it forms a soft dough.*

*Using a sharp knife, make deep cuts to
form 8 portions.*

CHEESE AND HERB PULL-APART LOAF

Preparation time: 25 minutes
+ 1 hour 40 minutes rising
Total cooking time: 30 minutes
Serves 6–8

7 g (¼ oz) dried yeast
1 teaspoon sugar
4 cups (500 g/1 lb) plain flour
1½ teaspoons salt
2 tablespoons chopped fresh parsley
2 tablespoons chopped fresh chives
1 tablespoon chopped fresh thyme
60 g (2 oz) cheddar cheese, grated

1 Combine the yeast, sugar and ½ cup (125 ml/4 fl oz) of warm water in a small bowl. Cover and set aside in a warm place for 10 minutes, or until frothy.

2 Sift the flour and salt into a bowl. Make a well in the centre and pour in 1 cup (250 ml/8 fl oz) warm water and the frothy yeast. Mix to a soft dough. Knead on a lightly floured surface for 10 minutes, or until smooth. Put the dough in an oiled bowl, cover loosely with greased plastic wrap and leave for 1 hour, or until doubled in size.

3 Punch down and knead for 1 minute. Divide the dough in half and shape each half into 10 flat discs, 6 cm (2½ inches) in diameter. Mix the fresh herbs with the cheddar and put 2 teaspoons on a disc. Press another disc on top. Repeat with the remaining discs and herb mixture.

4 Grease a 21 x 10.5 x 6.5 cm (8½ x 4¼ x 2½ inch) loaf tin. Stand the filled discs upright in the prepared tin, squashing them together. Cover the tin with a damp tea towel and set aside in a warm place for 30 minutes, or until well risen. Preheat the oven to hot 210°C (415°F/Gas 6–7).

5 Glaze with a little milk and bake the loaf for 30 minutes, or until brown and crusty.

Working on a lightly floured surface, flatten the dough into flat discs.

Spoon the filling onto one disc and top with another, pressing down firmly.

Stand the discs upright in the loaf tin, squashing them together.

TOMATO HERB ROLLS

Preparation time: 30 minutes
+ 1 hour 35 minutes rising
Total cooking time: 35 minutes
Makes 12 rolls

7 g (¼ oz) dried yeast
1 teaspoon sugar
4 cups (500 g/l lb) plain flour
1 teaspoon salt
2 cloves garlic, finely chopped
½ cup (75 g/2½ oz) sun-dried
   tomatoes, finely chopped
1 tablespoon chopped fresh oregano

1 tablespoon chopped fresh
   marjoram
1 tablespoon chopped fresh thyme
2 tablespoons chopped fresh flat-leaf
   parsley
30 g (1 oz) butter, melted
½ cup (125 ml/4 fl oz) milk, plus
   extra, to glaze

1 Mix the yeast, sugar and ½ cup
(125 ml/4 fl oz) of warm water in a
bowl. Set aside for 10 minutes, or until
frothy. Sift flour and salt into a bowl;
make a well in the centre.
2 Mix in the garlic, sun-dried
tomato and herbs. Pour in the melted
butter, frothy yeast and milk and mix

to a soft dough. Knead on a lightly
floured surface for 10 minutes, or
until smooth. Cover loosely with
greased plastic wrap and leave for 45
minutes, or until well risen.
3 Punch down and knead for 5
minutes. Divide into twelve and roll
into balls. Lay apart on a greased
baking tray. Leave for 30 minutes, or
until well risen. Preheat the oven to
hot 210°C (415°F/Gas 6–7). Brush
the rolls with milk and bake for 10
minutes. Reduce the oven to 180°C
(350°F/Gas 4) and bake for 20–25
minutes, or until the rolls are golden.

*Add the garlic, sun-dried tomato and
herbs to the flour mixture.*

*Using a sharp floured knife, divide the
dough into 12 equal portions.*

*The rolls are cooked when the bases
sound hollow when tapped.*

OLIVE SPIRALS

Preparation time: 25 minutes
+ 1 hour 30 minutes rising
Total cooking time: 35 minutes
Makes 12 spirals

7 g (¼ oz) dried yeast
1 teaspoon sugar
4 cups (600 g/1¼ lb) plain flour
1 teaspoon salt
2 tablespoons olive oil
2 cups (250 g/8 oz) pitted black olives
½ cup (50 g/1¾ oz) finely grated
   parmesan
3 cloves garlic, chopped

1 Mix the yeast, sugar and ½ cup (125 ml/4 fl oz) of warm water in a bowl. Cover and set aside in a warm place for 10 minutes, or until the mixture has become frothy.
2 Sift the flour and salt into a bowl and make a well in the centre. Add the frothy yeast, oil and 1 cup (250 ml/8 fl oz) of warm water. Mix to a soft dough and gather into a ball. Turn out onto a floured surface and knead for 10 minutes, or until smooth. Cover loosely with greased plastic wrap and set aside for 1 hour, or until well risen.
3 Process the olives, parmesan and garlic in a food processor until chopped. With the motor still running, add 1 tablespoon of oil and process to a paste.
4 Punch down the dough and knead for 1 minute. Roll out to a rectangle 42 x 35 cm (18 x 14 inches). Spread with the olive paste, leaving a plain strip along one of the long sides. Roll up lengthways, ending with the plain long side.
5 Cut into 12 slices and place close together on a greased baking tray. Cover with a damp tea towel and set aside for 30 minutes, or until well risen. Preheat the oven to 200°C (400°F/Gas 6). Bake for 35 minutes, or until golden brown.

Spread with olive paste and roll up lengthways.

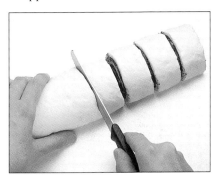

Using a serrated knife, cut the logs into 12 equal slices.

Place the spirals close together on the baking tray.

CARAMELISED ONION BRAIDS

Preparation time: 1 hour
+ 1 hour 35 minutes rising
Total cooking time: 1 hour
35 minutes
Serves 8–10

2½ cups (310 g/10 oz) plain flour
1 cup (130 g/4¼ oz) buckwheat flour
1 teaspoon salt
15 g (½ oz) fresh yeast or
   7 g (¼ oz) dried yeast
1¼ cups (315 ml/10 fl oz) warm milk
30 g (1 oz) butter
1 tablespoon oil
1 kg (2 lb) onions, thinly sliced into
   rings
1 egg, lightly beaten
2 teaspoons fennel seeds

1 Sift the flours and salt into a large bowl make a well in the centre. Dissolve the yeast in ½ cup (125 ml/4 fl oz) of the warm milk in a small bowl. Add the remaining warm milk. Pour into the well and mix to a dough. Turn out the dough out onto a floured surface and knead for 8 minutes, or until smooth. Place in a large oiled bowl, cover loosely with greased plastic wrap. Leave in a warm place for 45 minutes–1 hour, or until doubled in size.
2 Melt the butter and oil in a frying pan. Add the onion and cook over medium-low heat for approximately 40–50 minutes, or until the onion is golden.
3 Punch down the dough, turn out onto a lightly floured surface and knead for 10 minutes, or until smooth and elastic.

4 Lightly grease 2 baking trays. Divide the dough in half. Working with 1 piece at a time, divide it into 3 pieces. Roll each piece out to a 30 x 10 cm (12 x 4 inch) rectangle. Divide the onion mixture into 6 portions and spread a portion along the middle of each rectangle, leaving a 2 cm (¾ inch) border. Brush the edge with some of the beaten egg and roll over lengthways to enclose the filling.
5 Plait the 3 pieces together and place seam-side-down on a baking

tray. Pinch the ends together. Repeat with the remaining dough and caramelised onion. Cover with a damp tea towel and leave in a warm place for 45 minutes, or until well risen.
6 Preheat the oven to moderate 180°C (350°F/Gas 4). Brush the top with the beaten egg and sprinkle with the fennel seeds. Bake for 35–45 minutes, or until well browned. Transfer to a wire rack to cool.

On a lightly floured surface, roll each portion out into a rectangle.

Brush the edge with the beaten egg and roll over to enclose the filling.

Plait the 3 pieces together. Place seam-side-down on a baking tray.

WALNUT BREAD

Preparation time: 20 minutes
+ 1 hour 40 minutes rising
Total cooking time: 40 minutes
Serves 8–10

1½ cups (185 g/6 oz) chopped walnuts
7 g (¼ oz) dried yeast
1 teaspoon sugar
2 cups (250 g/8 oz) plain flour
1 cup (150 g/5 oz) wholemeal plain flour
1 cup (100 g/3½ oz) rye flour
1 teaspoon salt
1 tablespoon plain flour, extra

1 Lay the walnuts on a baking tray and bake in a moderate 180°C (350°F/Gas 4) oven for 5 minutes, or until lightly toasted. Set aside to cool.
2 Mix the yeast, sugar and ½ cup (125 ml/4 fl oz) of warm water in a bowl. Cover and set aside in a warm place for 10 minutes, or until frothy.
3 Combine the flours, salt and walnuts in a large bowl. Make a well in the centre and pour in another 1 cup (250 ml/8 fl oz) of warm water and the frothy yeast. Mix with a flat-bladed knife to a soft dough and gather into a ball. Turn out onto a lightly floured surface and knead for

10 minutes, or until smooth and elastic.
4 Place into a large, lightly oiled bowl, cover loosely with greased plastic wrap and leave for 1 hour, or until slightly risen.
5 Knead for 1 minute. Divide in half and form into 2 rounds 2.5 cm (1 inch) thick. Lay on a floured baking tray and cover with a damp tea towel. Set aside in a warm place for 30 minutes.
6 Sprinkle the top of the loaves with the extra flour by hand or with a sifter. Using a sharp knife, slash the dough diagonally. Bake for 35 minutes, or until crusty and brown.

Bake the chopped walnuts on a baking tray until lightly toasted.

Shape each half into a round. Place on a lightly floured baking tray.

Sprinkle the loaves with the extra flour by hand or use a sifter.

149

BEER BREAD WITH SUN-DRIED TOMATO AND HERBS

Preparation time: 20 minutes
Total cooking time: 45 minutes
Makes one loaf

1 tablespoon finely chopped fresh oregano, or 1½ teaspoons dried
¼ cup finely chopped fresh parsley
2 tablespoons finely chopped fresh basil
¼ cup chopped sun-dried tomato
1 teaspoon cracked black pepper
¼ cup grated parmesan cheese
2 cloves garlic, crushed
3 cups self-raising flour
1 teaspoon salt
2 teaspoons sugar
1½ cups beer (not bitter), at room temperature
2 teaspoons olive oil

1 Preheat oven to moderately hot 210°C (190°C gas). Brush 25 x 15 x 5.5 cm loaf tin with melted butter. Combine oregano, parsley, basil, sun-dried tomato, pepper, cheese and garlic in a small mixing bowl.
2 Sift flour, salt and sugar into a large mixing bowl. Make a well in the centre, add herb mixture and beer. Stir with a wooden spoon for 1 minute. (The mixture should be very moist; add a little more beer if necessary.)
3 Spoon the mixture into prepared tin; smooth surface. Bake for 10 minutes, reduce heat to moderate 180°C, bake 30 more minutes; brush top of loaf with oil, cook for 5 more minutes or until well browned and cooked through. Turn onto a wire rack to cool.

COOK'S FILE

Storage time: This bread is best eaten on the day it is baked.

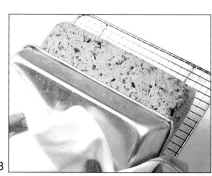

LEMON PEPPER DAMPER

Preparation time: 18 minutes
Total cooking time: 25 minutes
Serves 6–8

2 cups self-raising flour
1 teaspoon salt
2 teaspoons lemon pepper, or
  1 teaspoon grated lemon rind
  and 2 teaspoons black pepper
45 g butter, chopped
1 tablespoon chopped fresh chives
¾ cup grated cheddar cheese

2 teaspoons white vinegar
¾ cup milk

1 Preheat oven to moderately hot 210°C (190°C gas). Brush an oven tray with melted butter or oil. Sift flour and salt into a large bowl and add lemon pepper, or lemon rind and pepper. Using fingertips, rub in butter until mixture resembles coarse breadcrumbs. Stir in chives and cheese.

2 Stir vinegar into milk (it should look slightly curdled). Add to the flour and mix to a soft dough; add a little more milk if dough is too stiff.

3 Turn dough onto a lightly floured surface and knead until smooth. Place on prepared tray and press out into a circle approximately 2.5 cm thick. Mark with a knife into 8 wedges, cutting lightly into the top of damper. Dust top lightly with flour. Bake for 25 minutes, or until damper is deep golden and sounds hollow when tapped on the base. Serve warm with butter.

COOK'S FILE

Storage time: Damper is best eaten as soon as it is cooked.

CORN MUFFINS

Preparation time: 20 minutes
Total cooking time: 25 minutes
Makes 12

2½ cups (310 g/10 oz) self-raising
flour
½ cup (75 g/2½ oz) cornmeal
1 cup (250 ml/8 fl oz) milk
125 g (4 oz) butter, melted
2 eggs, lightly beaten
130 g (4½ oz) can corn kernels,
    drained
2 spring onions, finely chopped
½ cup (60 g/2 oz) grated cheddar
    cheese

1 Preheat the oven to hot 210°C
(415°F/Gas 6–7). Grease two trays
of six ½-cup (125 ml/4 fl oz) muffin
holes with butter. Sift the flour and
cornmeal into a large bowl and make
a well in the centre.
2 Whisk together the milk, butter,
eggs, corn, spring onion, cheddar
and salt and pepper in a separate
bowl and pour into the well. Fold
gently with a metal spoon until all
the ingredients are just combined.
Do not overmix—the mixture should
still be very lumpy.
3 Spoon the mixture into the tin
and bake for 20–25 minutes, or until
lightly golden. Leave for 5 minutes
before removing from the tin. Serve
split in half spread with butter or
cream cheese. Delicious warm or at
room temperature.

COOK'S FILE

Variation: Muffins are so versatile, you
can virtually add whatever you have in
the cupboard. Try adding 2 tablespoons
chopped chives, ¼ cup (40 g/1¼ oz)
chopped, drained sun-dried tomatoes
or capsicum in oil, 2 finely chopped
rashers of bacon, 2 finely chopped red
chillies or ½ finely chopped red or green
capsicum into the mixture with the milk
and Cheddar. Another delicious
variation is to sprinkle sesame or
sunflower seeds over the muffins just
before baking.Storage time: Store the
muffins in an airtight container for up
to 2 days.

*Using a sharp knife, finely chop the
spring onions.*

*Sift the flour and cornmeal into a large
bowl and make a well in the centre.*

*Pour in the milk mixture and fold gently
until just combined.*

*Spoon the dough into the muffin holes
and bake until lightly golden.*

CHEESE STICKS

Preparation time: 20 minutes
+ 20 minutes refrigeration
Total cooking time: 10 minutes
Makes 30

1¼ cups (155 g/5 oz) plain flour
100 g (3½ oz) unsalted butter, chilled
  and chopped
¾ cup (100 g/3½ oz) grated gruyère
1 tablespoon finely chopped fresh
  oregano
1 egg yolk
1 tablespoon sea salt flakes

1 Line two baking trays with baking paper. Put the flour and butter in a food processor and process in short bursts until the mixture resembles fine breadcrumbs. Add the gruyère and oregano and process for 5–10 seconds, or until just combined. Add the egg yolk and about 1 tablespoon water, and process until the dough just comes together.
2 Turn out onto a lightly floured surface and gather into a ball. Form two teaspoons of dough into a ball and then roll out into a stick about 12 cm (5 inches) long and place on the baking trays. Repeat with the remaining dough, then cover with plastic wrap and refrigerate for

15–20 minutes. Preheat the oven to moderately hot 200°C (400°F/Gas 6).
3 Lightly brush the sticks with water and sprinkle with the sea salt flakes. Bake for 10 minutes, or until golden. Cool on a wire rack and serve with dips or as part of an antipasto platter.

COOK'S FILE

Storage time: Cheese sticks will keep for up to 1 week in an airtight container.

Add the egg yolk and a little water and process until the dough clumps together.

Roll the balls of dough into sticks about 12 cm (5 inches) long.

Brush the sticks with water and sprinkle with sea salt flakes before baking.

153

DIPS

HUMMUS

Preparation time: 20 minutes
+ overnight soaking
Total cooking time: 1 hour
15 minutes
Makes 3 cups

1 cup (220 g) dried chickpeas
2 tablespoons tahini
4 cloves garlic, crushed
2 teaspoons ground cumin
⅓ cup (80 ml) lemon juice
3 tablespoons olive oil
large pinch cayenne pepper
extra lemon juice, optional
extra olive oil, to garnish
paprika, to garnish
chopped fresh parsley, to garnish

1 Soak the chickpeas in 1 litre water overnight. Drain and place in a large saucepan with 2 litres fresh water (enough to cover the chickpeas by 5 cm). Bring to the boil, then reduce the heat and simmer for 1 hour 15 minutes, or until the chickpeas are very tender. Skim any scum from the surface. Drain well, reserve the cooking liquid and leave until cool enough to handle. Pick over for any loose skins and discard.

2 Process the chickpeas, tahini, garlic, cumin, lemon juice, olive oil, cayenne pepper and 1½ teaspoons salt in a food processor until thick and smooth. With the motor still running, gradually add enough reserved cooking liquid (about ¾ cup/185 ml) to form a smooth creamy purée. Season with salt or extra lemon juice.

3 Spread onto a flat bowl or plate, drizzle with oil, sprinkle with paprika and scatter the parsley over the top. Serve the hummus with pitta bread or pide.

Pick through the cooled chickpeas to remove any loose skins.

Process the chickpea mix with the reserved cooking liquid until creamy.

CHILLI CRAB AND TOMATO DIP

Preparation time: 25 minutes
Total cooking time: Nil
Serves 6

2 x 170 g (5½ oz) cans crab meat, drained
200 g (6½ oz) neufchatel cheese (see Note)
2 tablespoons chilli sauce
2 teaspoons tomato paste
1 teaspoon grated lemon rind
2 teaspoons lemon juice
1 small onion, finely grated
3 spring onions, finely sliced
1 tomato, seeded and finely chopped

1 Squeeze any remaining liquid from the crab meat. Beat the neufchatel until smooth, then add the crab meat, chilli sauce, tomato paste, lemon rind, lemon juice and onion. Season well with salt and pepper. Mix together well and spoon into a serving bowl.
2 Scatter the spring onion and chopped tomato over the top and chill before serving.

COOK'S FILE
Note: Neufchatel is a smooth, mild, good-quality cream cheese available from delicatessens.

Squeeze any remaining liquid from the crab or the dip will be watery.

Beat the neufchatel cheese with a wooden spoon until it is smooth.

Add the crab meat, chilli sauce, tomato paste, lemon rind and juice, and onion.

TARAMOSALATA

Preparation time: 10 minutes
+ 10 minutes soaking
Total cooking time: Nil
Makes 1½ cups

5 slices white bread, crusts removed
⅓ cup (80 ml) milk
100 g can tarama (mullet roe)
1 egg yolk

½ small onion, grated
1 clove garlic, crushed
2 tablespoons lemon juice
⅓ cup (80 ml) olive oil
pinch ground white pepper

1 Soak the bread in the milk for 10 minutes. Press in a strainer to extract any excess milk, then place in a food processor with the tarama, egg yolk, onion and garlic. Process for 30 seconds, or until smooth, then add 1 tablespoon lemon juice.

2 With the motor running, slowly pour in the olive oil. The mixture should be smooth and of a dipping consistency. Add the remaining lemon juice and a pinch of white pepper. If the dip tastes too salty, add another piece of bread.

COOK'S FILE
Variation: Try smoked cod's roe instead of the mullet roe.

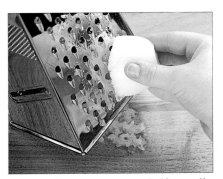

Using a cheese grater, grate half a small onion.

Press the soaked bread pieces in a strainer to extract any excess milk.

Process the bread, tarama, egg yolk, onion and garlic until smooth.

BABA GHANNOUJ

Preparation time: 20 minutes
+ 30 minutes cooling
Total cooking time: 50 minutes
Makes 1¾ cups

2 eggplants (1 kg)
3 cloves garlic, crushed
½ teaspoon ground cumin
⅓ cup (80 ml) lemon juice
2 tablespoons tahini
pinch cayenne pepper
1½ tablespoons olive oil
1 tablespoon finely chopped
    fresh flat-leaf parsley
black olives, to garnish

1 Preheat the oven to moderately
hot 200°C (400°F/Gas 6). Pierce the
eggplants several times with a fork,
then cook over an open flame for
about 5 minutes, or until the skin
is black and blistering, then place
in a roasting tin and bake for
40–45 minutes, or until the eggplants
are very soft and wrinkled. Place in
a colander over a bowl to drain off
any bitter juices and leave to stand
for 30 minutes, or until cool.
2 Carefully peel the skin from the
eggplant, chop the flesh and place
in a food processor with the garlic,
cumin, lemon, tahini, cayenne and
olive oil. Process until smooth and
creamy. Alternatively, use a potato
masher or fork. Season with salt and
stir in the parsley. Spread onto a flat
bowl or plate and garnish with the
olives. Serve with flatbread or pide.

COOK'S FILE

Note: If you prefer, you can simply roast
the eggplant in a roasting tin in a
moderately hot (200°C/400°F/Gas 6)
oven for 1 hour, or until very soft and
wrinkled. Eggplants are also known
as aubergines. The name baba
ghannouj is roughly translated as
'poor man's caviar'.

*Carefully peel the skin away from the
baked eggplant.*

*Process the eggplant, garlic, cumin,
lemon, tahini, cayenne and olive oil.*

TZATZIKI

Preparation time: 10 minutes
+ 15 minutes standing
Total cooking time: Nil
Makes 2 cups

2 Lebanese cucumbers (about 300 g)
400 g Greek-style plain yoghurt
4 cloves garlic, crushed
3 tablespoons finely chopped fresh
    mint, plus extra to garnish
1 tablespoon lemon juice

1   Cut the cucumbers in half lengthways, scoop out the seeds and discard. Leave the skin on and coarsely grate the cucumber into a small colander. Sprinkle with salt and leave over a large bowl for 15 minutes to drain off any bitter juices.
2   Meanwhile, place the Greek-style yoghurt, crushed garlic, mint and lemon juice in a bowl, and stir until well combined.
3   Rinse the cucumber under cold water then, taking small handfuls, squeeze out any excess moisture. Combine the grated cucumber with the yoghurt mixture then season to taste with salt and freshly ground black pepper. Serve immediately or refrigerate until ready to serve, garnished with the extra mint.

COOK'S FILE
Note: Tzatziki is often served as a dip with flatbread or Turkish pide but is also suitable to serve as a sauce to accompany seafood and meat.
Storage: Tzatziki will keep in an airtight container in the refrigerator for 2–3 days.

Cut the cucumbers in half and scoop out the seeds with a teaspoon.

Mix the yoghurt, garlic, mint and lemon juice together.

Squeeze the grated cucumber to remove any excess moisture.

GUACAMOLE

Preparation time: 30 minutes
Total cooking time: Nil
Serves 6

3 ripe avocados
1 tablespoon lime or lemon juice
1 tomato
1–2 red chillies, finely chopped
1 small red onion, finely chopped
1 tablespoon finely chopped
    coriander leaves
2 tablespoons sour cream
1–2 drops Tabasco or habanero sauce

1 Roughly chop the avocado flesh
and place in a bowl. Mash lightly
with a fork and sprinkle with the
lime or lemon juice to prevent the
avocado discolouring.
2 Cut the tomato in half horizontally
and use a teaspoon to scoop out the
seeds. Finely dice the flesh and add
to the avocado.
3 Stir in the chilli, onion, coriander,
sour cream and Tabasco or habanero
sauce. Season with freshly cracked
black pepper.
4 Serve immediately or cover
the surface with plastic wrap and
refrigerate for 1–2 hours. If refrigerated, leave at room temperature for
15 minutes before serving.

COOK'S FILE

Hint: You will need 1–2 limes to produce
1 tablespoon of juice, depending on the
lime. A heavier lime will probably be
more juicy. To get more juice from a
citrus fruit, prick it all over with a fork
and then heat on High (100%) in the
microwave for 1 minute. Don't forget to
prick it or the fruit may burst.

*Use disposable gloves when chopping
chilli to avoid skin irritation.*

*Remove the avocado stone by chopping
into it with a sharp knife and lifting up.*

*Cut the tomato in half horizontally and
scoop out the seeds with a teaspoon.*

*You will only need a couple of drops of
Tabasco or habanero—they are very hot.*

BEETROOT HUMMUS

Preparation time: 15 minutes
Total cooking time: 40 minutes
Serves 8 (Makes 2 cups)

500 g beetroot, trimmed
⅓ cup (80 ml) olive oil
1 large onion, chopped
1 tablespoon ground cumin
400 g can chickpeas, drained
1 tablespoon tahini
⅓ cup (80 g) plain yoghurt
3 cloves garlic, crushed
¼ cup (60 ml) lemon juice
½ cup (125 ml) vegetable stock

1 Scrub the beetroot well. Bring a large saucepan of water to the boil over high heat and cook the beetroot for 35–40 minutes, or until soft and cooked through. Drain and cool slightly before peeling.
2 Meanwhile, heat 1 tablespoon of the oil in a frying pan over medium heat and cook the onion for 2–3 minutes, or until soft. Add the cumin and cook for a further 1 minute, or until fragrant.
3 Chop the beetroot and place in a food processor or blender with the onion mixture, chickpeas, tahini, yoghurt, garlic, lemon juice and stock and process until smooth. With the motor running, add the remaining oil in a thin steady stream. Process until

the mixture is thoroughly combined. Serve the hummus with Lebanese or Turkish bread.

COOK'S FILE

Note: Beetroot hummus can be a great accompaniment to a main meal or is delicious as part of a meze platter with bruschetta or crusty bread. Its vivid colour sparks up any table.
Variation: You can use 500 g of any vegetable to make the hummus. Try carrot or pumpkin.

Drain and cool the beetroots, then peel off the skins.

Cook the onion and cumin for 1 minute, or until fragrant.

Blend all the hummus ingredients until smooth.

PESTO

Preparation time: 10 minutes
Total cooking time: 2 minutes
Makes 1 cup

50 g pine nuts
50 g small fresh basil leaves
2 cloves garlic, crushed
½ teaspoon sea salt
½ cup (125 ml) olive oil
30 g parmesan, finely grated
20 g pecorino cheese, finely grated

1   Preheat the oven to moderate 180°C (350°F/Gas 4). Spread the pine nuts on a baking tray and bake for 2 minutes, or until lightly golden. Cool.
2   Place the pine nuts, basil, garlic, salt and oil in a food processor and process until smooth. Transfer to a bowl and stir in the cheeses until well combined. Serve with a meze plate, pasta, meat or soup.

COOK'S FILE
Note: Pesto is one of the most famous Italian sauces and is served with many dishes including chicken and fish.

Bake the pine nuts in a moderate oven until lightly golden.

Process the pine nuts, basil, garlic, sea salt and oil until smooth.

Stir the parmesan and pecorino into the basil mixture.

ROASTED CAPSICUM AND CHILLI DIP

Preparation time: 40 minutes
+ 30 minutes refrigeration
Total cooking time: 35 minutes
Serves 8

2 large red capsicums
3 tablespoons olive oil
1–2 birds-eye chillies
200 g (6½ oz) neufchatel cream
   cheese
3 tablespoons thick plain yoghurt
1 teaspoon red wine vinegar
½ teaspoon soft brown sugar
2 spring onions, chopped

1 Preheat the oven to moderately hot 200°C (400°F/Gas 6). Put the capsicums in a baking dish and drizzle with oil. Bake for 15 minutes. Make a small slit in each of the whole chillies (otherwise they will explode), add to the dish and bake for a further 20 minutes. (If the vegetables begin to burn, add about 1 tablespoon of water to the baking dish.) Allow to cool.
2 Peel the skin from the cooled capsicums. Cut them and the chillies in half and discard the seeds and membrane. Place the capsicum and chillies in a food processor and mix until pulpy.
3 Beat the cream cheese until soft, then add the capsicum chilli mixture, yoghurt, vinegar and sugar. Season to taste with salt and pepper, then cover and refrigerate for 30 minutes. Scatter with the spring onions to serve.

Roast the capsicums for 15 minutes, then add the chillies.

Put the capsicum and chillies in a food processor and mix until pulpy.

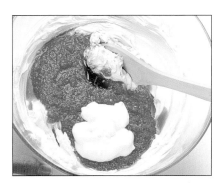

Mix together all the ingredients, then refrigerate for 30 minutes before serving.

QUICK DIPS

Informal food suited to eating outdoors often forms the basis of barbecues. These easy-to-make dips are instant crowd-pleasers and make casual but delicious accompaniments to cooked meat and salads.

ROSEMARY AND CANNELLINI BEAN DIP

Rinse and drain a 400 g (13 oz) can cannellini beans. Place the beans in a food processor with 1 crushed clove garlic, 2 teaspoons chopped rosemary and 1 tablespoon lemon juice. Process for 1 minute, or until smooth. With the motor running add 2 tablespoons extra virgin olive oil in a thin stream. Season with salt and pepper and serve at room temperature with crisp lavash bread or pitta chips. Serves 4.

FRENCH ONION DIP

Place 250 g (8 oz) sour cream in a small bowl. Add a 30 g (1 oz) packet French onion soup mix and blend well with a fork. Cover with plastic wrap and refrigerate for 1–2 hours. Serve with potato wedges, sweet potato chips or savoury biscuits. Serves 4.

SWEET CHILLI AND SOUR CREAM DIP

Mix 250 g (8 oz) sour cream with 3 tablespoons sweet chilli sauce. Swirl another teaspoon of sweet chilli sauce on top to decorate. Serve with herb and garlic pitta chips, goujons or sweet potato chips. Serves 4.

MIXED HERB DIP

Chop 15 g ($^1/_2$ oz) chives into short lengths and mix with 1$^1/_4$ cups (315 ml/10 fl oz) plain yoghurt. Add $^1/_4$ cup (7 g/$^1/_4$ oz) whole marjoram leaves, $^1/_4$ cup (5 g/$^1/_4$ oz) mint leaves and $^1/_2$ cup (10 g/$^1/_4$ oz) flat-leaf parsley leaves. Season with cracked black pepper. Serve with crisp lavash bread, pitta or sweet chilli chips. Try other fresh herbs such as thyme, oregano, dill or garlic chives. Serves 6.

RED PESTO DIP

Mix together 250 g (8 oz) soft cream cheese, 2 tablespoons ready-made red pesto, 1 teaspoon lemon juice and 2 teaspoons chopped flat-leaf parsley. Season with black pepper and serve with herb and garlic pitta chips or savoury biscuits. Serves 4.

MUSTARD DIP

Mix together $^1/_2$ cup (125 g/4 fl oz) mayonnaise, $^1/_2$ cup (125 g/4 fl oz) plain yoghurt, 2 teaspoons Dijon mustard and 3 tablespoons wholegrain mustard. Season well and serve with chicken goujons or potato wedges. Serves 4.

CREAMY TOMATO TUNA DIP

Put 250 g (8 oz) soft cream cheese and 100 g (6½ oz) can tuna with tomato and onion in a small bowl and mix well with a fork. Don't drain the oil from the tuna as it boosts the flavour and gives the dip a smooth texture. Season with freshly cracked black pepper, cover with plastic wrap and refrigerate for 1–2 hours. Serve with sweet chilli chips, crisp lavash bread or potato wedges. A variety of different flavoured canned tunas are available. Try tuna with tomato and basil, or tuna with herbs and garlic. Serves 4.

HUMMUS AND ORANGE DIP

Mix together 250 g (8 oz) hummus, 2 tablespoons orange juice, ¼ teaspoon ground cumin and 2 teaspoons chopped coriander. Season with freshly cracked black pepper and cover with plastic wrap. Refrigerate for 2–3 hours to develop the flavours. Serve with sweet potato chips, crisp lavash bread or pitta chips. Serves 4.

Top, from left: Hummus and Orange; Red Pesto; Mixed Herb; French Onion. Bottom, from left: Mustard; Sweet Chilli and Sour Cream; Creamy Tomato Tuna; Rosemary and Cannellini Bean.

SALSAS AND SAUCES

MEXICAN SALSA

Preparation time: 40 minutes
+ overnight standing
Total cooking time: 1 hour
Serves 10–12

250 g (8 oz) black-eyed beans
250 g (8 oz) red kidney beans
500 g (1 lb) sweet potato
1 large red onion, chopped
1 large green capsicum, chopped
3 ripe tomatoes, chopped
¼ cup (15 g/½ oz) chopped
   fresh basil
3 flour tortillas
1 tablespoon oil
2 tablespoons grated parmesan

DRESSING

1 clove garlic, crushed
1 tablespoon lime juice
2 tablespoons olive oil

1 Soak the beans in a large bowl of cold water overnight. Drain and cook in a large pan of rapidly boiling water for 30 minutes, or until just tender. Skim off any scum that appears on the surface during cooking. Do not overcook or they will become mushy. Drain and set aside to cool.
2 Chop the sweet potato into large pieces and cook in boiling water until tender. Drain and combine with the onion, capsicum, tomato and beans. Stir in the basil.
3 To make the Dressing, shake the ingredients in a jar until combined. Pour over the salsa and toss to coat.
4 Preheat the oven to 180°C (350°F/ Gas 4). Using a small knife, cut cactus shapes or large triangles out of the tortillas, brush lightly with the oil and sprinkle with parmesan. Bake for 5–10 minutes, or until crisp and golden.
5 Put the salsa in a large bowl or on a platter and arrange the cactus shapes on top.

COOK'S FILE

Hint: Top the salsa with some soured cream and guacamole, if desired.

Combine the sweet potato with the onion, capsicum, tomato and beans.

Using a small sharp knife, cut cactus shapes out of the tortillas.

CHARGRILLED VEGETABLE SALSA

Preparation time: 30 minutes
+ 2 hours marinating
Total cooking time: 30 minutes
Serves 4

2 Roma tomatoes
1 small red capsicum
1 small green capsicum
2 small zucchini
2 slender eggplants
3 tablespoons olive oil
1 tablespoon chopped fresh
    flat-leaf parsley
2 teaspoons chopped fresh marjoram
2 teaspoons chopped fresh oregano
2 tablespoons balsamic vinegar
1 tablespoon chopped fresh flat-leaf
    parsley, extra
2 teaspoons chopped fresh
    marjoram, extra

1 Halve the tomatoes, capsicums, zucchini and eggplants lengthways. Place in a large shallow dish and pour over the combined olive oil and herbs. Toss well and leave to marinate for at least 2 hours or up to a day.
2 Heat the barbecue or chargrill pan and cook the vegetables until soft and a little blackened. Place the capsicum in a plastic bag for a few minutes, then peel away the skin. Cut all the vegetables into small pieces and mix with the vinegar and extra herbs.

Cut the tomatoes, capsicums, zucchini and eggplants in half lengthways.

Barbecue or chargrill the vegetables until soft and a little blackened.

Cut the vegetables into small chunks and mix with the herbs and vinegar.

PINEAPPLE SALSA

Preparation time: 20 minutes
+ 2 hours standing
Total cooking time: Nil
Serves 8

375 g (12 oz) pineapple, diced
1 small red onion, chopped
1 red capsicum, chopped
1 jalapeno chilli, seeded
1 tablespoon grated fresh ginger
finely grated rind of 1 lime

1 tablespoon lime juice
½ cup (15 g/½ oz) fresh coriander
  leaves, chopped

1 Put the diced pineapple, roughly chopped onion, capsicum, chilli and ginger in a food processor and mix, using the pulse button, until coarsely chopped. Stir in the lime rind and juice and the coriander leaves. Season, to taste, with salt and pour into a small bowl.
2 Cover and leave the salsa to stand for 2 hours. Drain off any excess liquid before serving.

Cut the skin from the pineapple with a sharp knife.

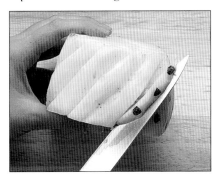

Cut out the tough eyes from the flesh of the pineapple.

Process the salsa until coarsely chopped then stir in the remaining ingredients.

BOCCONCINI, TOMATO AND SUN-DRIED CAPSICUM SALSA

Preparation time: 20 minutes
Total cooking time: Nil
Serves 6

180 g (6 oz) bocconcini, diced
200 g (6½ oz) tomatoes, diced
⅓ cup (50 g/1¾ oz) drained sun-
    dried capsicum in oil, chopped
1 spring onion, finely sliced
1 tablespoon extra virgin
    olive oil
2 teaspoons red wine vinegar

1 tablespoon shredded basil leaves
1 tablespoon chopped flat-leaf parsley

1 Mix together the bocconcini, tomato, sun-dried capsicum and spring onion in a large bowl.
2 Whisk together the oil and vinegar until thoroughly blended. Stir through the basil and parsley.
3 Toss the dressing through the bocconcini and tomato mixture and season to taste with salt and black pepper. Serve at room temperature.

COOK'S FILE
Note: Bocconcini are small, fresh mozzarella cheeses.

Cut the bocconcini cheese and tomatoes into small dice.

Mix together the bocconcini, tomato, capsicum and spring onion.

Stir the basil and flat-leaf parsley into the vinaigrette dressing.

RED CAPSICUM RELISH

Preparation time: 40 minutes
+ a few weeks standing
Total cooking time: 1 hour
45 minutes
Fills three 250 ml (8 fl oz) jars

1 kg (2 lb) red capsicums
1 teaspoon black peppercorns
2 teaspoons black mustard seeds
2 red onions, thinly sliced
4 cloves garlic, chopped
1½ cups (375 ml/12 fl oz) red wine
    vinegar
2 apples, peeled, cored and grated
1 teaspoon grated fresh ginger
1 cup (230 g/7½ oz) soft brown sugar

1 Cut the capsicums into quarters, remove the seeds and membrane and thinly slice. Tie the peppercorns in a piece of muslin and secure with string. Combine the capsicum, peppercorns, mustard seeds, onion, garlic, vinegar, apple and ginger in a large pan. Simmer for 30 minutes, or until the capsicum is soft.
2 Add the sugar and stir over low heat until completely dissolved. Simmer, stirring occasionally, for 1¼ hours, or until the relish has reduced and thickened. Remove the muslin bag.
3 Rinse the jars with boiling water then dry in a warm oven. Spoon the relish into the hot jars and seal. Turn the jars upside down for 2 minutes, then turn them the other way up and leave to cool. Label and date. Allow the flavours to develop for a few weeks before using. Will keep in a cool dark place for up to 1 year. Refrigerate after opening.

Put the peppercorns in the centre of a piece of muslin and tie with string.

Add the brown sugar to the capsicum mixture and stir over heat until dissolved.

Spoon the thickened relish into the sterilised jars and seal.

MEDITERRANEAN SALSA

Preparation time: 45 minutes
+ cooling
Total cooking time: 20 minutes
Serves 6

1 medium eggplant, diced
2 tablespoons olive oil
½ teaspoon salt
1 large red capsicum, diced
12 Kalamata olives, pitted and finely
    chopped
4 spring onions, finely chopped
1 small red chilli, chopped
2 cloves garlic, crushed
1 tablespoon olive oil
2 teaspoons red wine vinegar
2 teaspoons lemon juice
1 tablespoon chopped parsley
2 teaspoons chopped chives

1 Preheat the oven to moderate 180°C
(350°F/Gas 4). Toss the eggplant
with the olive oil and the salt, then
place in a single layer on a baking
tray. Cook for about 20 minutes, or
until golden and cooked. Remove
from the oven and allow to cool.
2 Gently mix the eggplant with the
capsicum, olives, spring onion, chilli,
garlic, olive oil, vinegar, lemon juice
and salt and freshly ground black
pepper, to taste.
3 Stir through the parsley and chives
and serve at room temperature.

COOK'S FILE

Note: Make sure the eggplant does not
have large hard or dark seeds—these
are unpalatable and will make the salsa
bitter. If you find them, cut them out
before roasting the eggplant.

*If you are very fond of olives, invest in
an olive pitter to make the task simple.*

*Toss the eggplant with the olive oil and
salt before roasting.*

*Add salt and pepper to the mixture, to
your taste.*

*Stir through the parsley and chives and
serve at room temperature.*

BEAN AND CHILLI SALSA

Preparation time: 20 minutes
+ 12 hours soaking
Total cooking time: 2 hours
45 minutes
Serves 8

¾ cup (150 g/5 oz) dried pinto beans
8 Roma tomatoes
1 tablespoon olive oil
3 red chillies, seeded and thinly sliced
2 cloves garlic, finely chopped
3 tablespoons lime juice
½ cup (15 g/½ oz) coriander leaves,
    finely chopped

1 Soak the beans in cold water for 12 hours or overnight.
2 Preheat the oven to moderate 180°C (350°F/Gas 4). Cut the tomatoes in half lengthways and place in a shallow baking dish. Drizzle with the oil and season well with salt and pepper. Cook for 2 hours, then cool slightly and cut into small pieces.
3 Drain and rinse the beans. Place in a large pan and cover with cold water. Bring to the boil and simmer for 40 minutes, or until tender. Drain and rinse well. Leave to cool.
4 Place the beans, tomato, chilli, garlic, lime juice and coriander in a bowl and mix until well combined.

Use rubber gloves when slicing chillies, to prevent skin irritation.

Cut the tomatoes in half lengthways and drizzle with the oil.

Simmer the beans for 40 minutes, or until they are tender.

Mix together all the salsa ingredients until they are well combined.

BARBECUE SAUCE

Preparation time: 15 minutes
Total cooking time: 10 minutes
Serves 4

2 teaspoons oil
1 small onion, finely chopped
1 tablespoon malt vinegar
1 tablespoon soft brown sugar
½ cup (80 ml/2¾ fl oz) tomato sauce

1 tablespoon Worcestershire
sauce

1 Heat the oil in a small pan and cook the onion over low heat for 3 minutes, or until soft, stirring occasionally.
2 Add the remaining ingredients and bring to the boil. Reduce the heat and simmer for 3 minutes, stirring occasionally. Serve warm or at room temperature. Can be kept, covered and refrigerated, for up to a week.

COOK'S FILE
Note: Shown here with a hamburger, this sauce is also a great accompaniment to just about any barbecued meat—chops, steak or sausages.

Chop the onion very finely so the sauce has a smooth texture.

Cook the onion over low heat, stirring occasionally, until soft.

Add the remaining ingredients to the pan and bring to the boil.

SATAY SAUCE

Preparation time: 10 minutes
Total cooking time: 15 minutes
Serves 8

1 tablespoon oil
1 large onion, finely chopped
2 cloves garlic, finely chopped
2 red chillies, finely chopped
1 teaspoon shrimp paste
250 g (8 oz) peanut butter
1 cup (250 ml/8 fl oz) coconut milk
2 teaspoons kecap manis or thick soy
    sauce
1 tablespoon tomato sauce

1 Heat the oil in a pan and cook the onion and garlic for 8 minutes over low heat, stirring regularly. Add the chilli and shrimp paste, cook for 1 minute and remove from the heat.
2 Add the peanut butter, return to the heat and stir in the coconut milk and 1 cup (250 ml/8 fl oz) water. Bring to the boil over low heat, stirring so that it does not stick. Add the kecap manis and tomato sauce and simmer for 1 minute. Cool.

COOK'S FILE

Note: Shown here with chicken skewers, this sauce is also excellent with meat or fish skewers.

Chop the chillies very finely. If you prefer a milder taste, remove the seeds first.

Cook the onion and garlic over low heat, then add the chilli and shrimp paste.

Bring to the boil, stirring, then add the kecap manis and tomato sauce.

LIME AND CHILLI SAUCE

Preparation time: 15 minutes
Total cooking time: Nil
Serves 4

¹/₂ cup (25 g/³/₄ oz) chopped and
firmly packed mint leaves
¹/₂ cup (25 g/³/₄ oz) chopped coriander
  leaves
1 teaspoon grated lime rind
1 tablespoon lime juice
1 teaspoon grated fresh ginger
1 jalapeno chilli, seeded and finely
  chopped
1 cup (250 g/8 oz) plain yoghurt

1 Mix together the mint, coriander, lime rind, lime juice, ginger and chilli. Fold in the yoghurt and season with salt and cracked pepper to taste.

COOK'S FILE

Note: Jalapeno chillies are smooth and thick-fleshed and are available both red and green. They are quite fiery and you can use a less powerful variety of chilli if you prefer.

It's a good idea to wear gloves to de-seed chillies, to prevent skin irritation.

Mix together the mint, coriander, lime rind, juice, ginger and chilli.

Check the taste of the sauce before seasoning with salt and black pepper.

BLACK BEAN SAUCE

Preparation time: 10 minutes
Total cooking time: 15 minutes
Serves 6

2 tablespoons salted black beans
1 tablespoon oil
1 small onion, finely chopped
1 tablespoon finely chopped fresh
   ginger
1 clove garlic, finely chopped
1 red chilli, seeded and finely chopped
1¼ cups (315 ml/10 fl oz) chicken
   stock
2 teaspoons cornflour
2 teaspoons sesame oil

1 Rinse the black beans under cold water for 3–4 minutes to remove any excess saltiness. Drain well.
2 Heat the oil in a small pan and add the onion, ginger, garlic and chilli. Cook over low heat until the onion is soft but not browned. Add the chicken stock and bring to the boil. Reduce the heat and simmer for 5 minutes.
3 Mix the cornflour and 1 tablespoon of water in a small bowl and add to the pan. Keep stirring and the mixture will thicken. Allow to simmer for 3 minutes, then add the beans and sesame oil and mix together well.

COOK'S FILE
Note: Black beans are available canned or in vacuum packs from Asian food stores. Don't confuse them with Mexican black turtle beans from health food shops. Shown here with grilled chicken, this sauce is also excellent with prawns or with barbecued salmon.

Rinse the black beans under running water to get rid of excess saltiness.

Cook until the onion is soft but not browned, then add the stock.

Simmer the sauce for 3 minutes, then stir in the beans and sesame oil.

CHILLI SPICED MANGO SAUCE

Preparation time: 35 minutes
Total cooking time: 20 minutes
Serves 4

1 large ripe mango
1 tablespoon oil
1 red onion, finely sliced
3 cloves garlic, finely chopped
4 cm (1½ inch) piece fresh ginger,
    finely chopped
2–3 red chillies, seeded and finely
    chopped
1 tablespoon honey
¼ teaspoon ground cinnamon
pinch of ground cardamom
pinch of ground nutmeg
pinch of ground cloves
¼ cup (60 ml/2 fl oz) dark rum
¼ cup (60 ml/2 fl oz) lime juice
¼ cup (7 g/¼ oz) coriander leaves,
    chopped

1 Peel the mango and dice the flesh.
Heat the oil in a frying pan and add
the onion, garlic, ginger and chilli.
Cook for about 3–4 minutes, or until
the onion is soft.
2 Add the mango, honey, cinnamon,
cardamom, nutmeg and cloves. Mix
well and bring to the boil. Simmer
gently for 5 minutes. Add the rum
and simmer for a further 5 minutes.
Add the lime juice, coriander and salt
and pepper to taste.

COOK'S FILE

Note: Shown here with chargrilled tuna,
this sauce is also good with chicken, or
another strong-flavoured fish such as
swordfish.

*Peel the mango and cut the flesh into
small cubes.*

*Fry the onion, garlic, ginger and chilli
until the onion is soft.*

*Add the rum to the simmering mixture
and cook for a further 5 minutes.*

SMOKY TOMATO SAUCE

Preparation time: 15 minutes
Total cooking time: 35–45
minutes
Makes about 1 litre

SMOKING MIX
2 tablespoons Chinese or
　Ceylon tea leaves
2 star anise, crushed
1 strip orange rind
½ teaspoon five-spice powder
6 juniper berries, crushed

2 onions, quartered
2 red capsicums, cut into large pieces
2 red chillies, cut in half
3 tablespoons oil
3 cloves garlic, chopped
500 g (1 lb) tomatoes, chopped
2 tablespoons Worcestershire sauce
½ cup (125 ml/4 fl oz) barbecue
　sauce
2 tablespoons tamarind concentrate
1 tablespoon white vinegar
1 tablespoon soft brown sugar

1 Combine all the ingredients for the smoking mix in a small bowl. Pour the mix into the centre of a sheet of foil and fold the edges to prevent the mix from spreading. (This will form an open container to allow the mix to smoke.) Place the foil container on the bottom of a dry wok or wide frying pan. Place an open rack or steamer in the wok or frying pan, making sure it is elevated over the mix.
2 Place the onion, capsicum and chilli onto the rack and cover them with a lid, or alternatively cover the entire wok or frying pan tightly with foil to prevent the smoke from escaping.

3 Smoke over medium heat for 10–15 minutes, or until the vegetables are tender. If you prefer a very smoky sauce cook the vegetables for longer, if you prefer it less so, reduce the time. Remove the container with the smoking mix.
4 Dice the onion, capsicum and chilli quite finely. Heat the oil in the wok and add the garlic and cooked vegetables. Fry over medium heat for 3 minutes, then add the tomato and cook until pulpy. Add the sauces, tamarind, vinegar and sugar. Simmer,

stirring occasionally, for 20–25 minutes, or until the sauce is quite thick. Serve with meat, fish or as a pasta sauce. Store in the refrigerator.

COOK'S FILE
Note: For a smoother sauce, process in a food processor for about 30 seconds.

Fold the edges of the foil to form an open container that allows the mix to smoke.

Place the open rack in the wok then put on the onion, capsicum and chilli.

Add the tamarind concentrate to the sauce and simmer.

DESSERTS

MANGO ICE CREAM IN BRANDY SNAP BASKETS

Preparation time: 15 minutes
+ freezing
Total cooking time: Nil
Serves 6

400 g frozen mango
½ cup (125 g) caster sugar
¼ cup (60 ml) mango or
    apricot nectar
300 ml cream
6 ready-made brandy snap baskets
mango slices, to garnish
fresh mint sprigs, to garnish

1 Defrost the mango until it is soft enough to mash but still icy. Place in a large bowl; add the sugar and mango nectar. Stir for 1–2 minutes, or until the sugar has dissolved.

2 Beat the cream in a bowl until stiff peaks form. Gently fold the cream into the mango mixture. Spoon the mixture into a deep tray or plastic container, cover and freeze for 1 hour 30 minutes, or until half-frozen. Quickly spoon the mixture into a food processor. Process for 30 seconds, or until smooth. Return to the tray, cover and freeze completely. Remove the ice cream from the freezer 10 minutes before serving, to allow it to soften a little. To serve, place 2 scoops ice cream in each brandy snap basket, and garnish with the mango slices and sprigs of mint.

COOK'S FILE

Hint: Freeze the ice cream for at least 8 hours before serving. It will keep in the freezer for up to 3 weeks. When available, use 3–4 fresh large mangoes and purée the flesh in a food processor.

FLOURLESS CHOCOLATE CAKE

Preparation time: 15 minutes
Total cooking time: 1 hour
Serves 8

½ cup (95 g) soft brown sugar
6 eggs
400 g dark chocolate
1 tablespoon Grand Marnier
1 teaspoon ground cinnamon
300 ml double thick cream, plus extra double thick cream, to serve
icing sugar, to dust
strawberries, to serve

1 Preheat the oven to moderate 180°C (350°F/Gas 4). Grease a 23 cm round cake tin and line the base with baking paper. Place the sugar and eggs in a bowl, and beat together for 10 minutes, or until creamy.
2 Meanwhile, chop the chocolate into small even-size pieces and place in a heatproof bowl. Bring a saucepan of water to the boil, then remove from the heat. Sit the bowl over the pan, making sure the base of the bowl does not touch the water. Stir occasionally until the chocolate has melted. Place the Grand Marnier, cinnamon, egg mixture and melted chocolate in a bowl and mix together. Stir the cream very gently by hand 2–3 times and then fold into the chocolate mixture.
3 Pour the mixture into the prepared tin and bake for 1 hour, or until a skewer comes out clean. Allow to cool in the tin, then turn out onto a cake rack when cold. Cut into slices, dust with icing sugar and serve with a dollop of cream and strawberries.

COOK'S FILE

Note: This is a moist cake and will sink a little in the middle. If you prefer, try using brandy, Tia Maria or Cointreau instead of Grand Marnier.

BROWNIES

Preparation time: 15 minutes
Total cooking time: 40 minutes
Makes 18

½ cup (60 g) self-raising flour
½ cup (60 g) plain flour
½ cup (60 g) cocoa powder
½ teaspoon bicarbonate of soda
1¼ cups (230 g) soft brown sugar
2 eggs
1 cup (250 ml) buttermilk
2 teaspoons vanilla essence
2 tablespoons oil
icing sugar, to dust

1 Preheat the oven to moderate 180°C (350°F/Gas 4). Lightly grease a 28 x 18 cm shallow tin and line the base with baking paper, extending over the two long sides.
2 Sift the flours, cocoa powder, bicarbonate of soda and a pinch of salt into a mixing bowl, then stir in the sugar. Whisk the eggs, buttermilk, vanilla and oil in a jug.
3 Gently stir the egg mixture into the dry ingredients until combined—do not overbeat. Pour into the tin and bake for 40 minutes, or until it springs back to a light touch in the centre. Leave in the tin for 5 minutes, then turn out onto a wire rack to cool completely.
4 To serve, cut into 18 squares and dust with icing sugar. Store in an airtight container for up to 3 days.

Line the tin with baking paper, leaving it hanging on the two long sides.

Gently stir the egg mixture into the dry ingredients until combined.

The brownies are cooked if the centre springs back when lightly touched.

LEMON GRANITA

Preparation time: 15 minutes
+ 2 hours freezing
Total cooking time: 5 minutes
Serves 6

1¼ cups (315 ml) lemon juice
1 tablespoon lemon zest
200 g caster sugar

1 Place the lemon juice, lemon zest and caster sugar in a small saucepan and stir over low heat for 5 minutes, or until sugar is dissolved. Remove from the heat and leave to cool.

2 Add 2 cups (500 ml) water to the juice mixture and mix together well. Pour the mixture into a shallow 30 x 20 cm metal container and place in the freezer until the mixture is beginning to freeze around the edges. Scrape the frozen sections back into the mixture with a fork. Repeat every 30 minutes until the mixture has even-size ice crystals. Beat the mixture with a fork just before serving. To serve, spoon the lemon granita into six chilled glasses.

Stir the juice, zest and sugar over low heat until the sugar has dissolved.

Scrape the frozen edges of the mixture back into the centre.

Beat the granita mixture with a fork just prior to serving.

WHITE CHOCOLATE CHEESECAKES WITH MIXED BERRIES

Preparation time: 15 minutes
+ 1 hour refrigeration
+ 15 minutes standing
Total cooking time: 25 minutes
Serves 4

4 butternut biscuits
75 g good-quality white chocolate
   buds
250 g cream cheese, at room
   temperature
¼ cup (60 ml) cream
½ cup (125 g) caster sugar
1 egg
250 g mixed berries, such as
   raspberries, blueberries and sliced
   strawberries
Framboise or Cointreau, optional

1 Preheat the oven to warm 160°C
(315°F/Gas 2–3). Grease four 1 cup
(250 ml) muffin holes and line with
2 strips of baking paper to make a
cross pattern. Put a biscuit in the
base of each hole. Place the chocolate
buds in a heatproof bowl. Bring a
saucepan of water to the boil, then
remove from the heat. Sit the bowl
over the pan, making sure the base
of the bowl does not sit in the water.
Stir occasionally until the chocolate
has melted.

2 Using electric beaters, beat the
cream cheese, cream and half the
sugar until thick and smooth. Beat in
the egg and then the melted chocolate.
Pour evenly into the muffin holes and
bake for 25 minutes, or until set. Cool
completely in the tin then carefully run
a small spatula or flat-bladed knife
around the edge and lift out of the
holes with the paper strips. Refrigerate
for 1 hour, or until ready to serve.

3 Place the berries in a bowl and
fold in the remaining sugar. Leave for
10–15 minutes, or until juices form.
Flavour with a little liqueur, such as
Framboise or Cointreau, if desired.
Serve the cheesecakes on individual
serving plates topped with the berries.

FRUIT KEBABS WITH HONEY CARDAMOM SYRUP

Preparation time: 15 minutes
+ 1 hour marinating
Total cooking time: 5 minutes
Makes 8 kebabs

1/4 small pineapple, peeled
1 peach

1 banana, peeled
16 strawberries

HONEY CARDAMOM SYRUP
2 tablespoons honey
20 g butter, melted
1/2 teaspoon ground cardamom
1 tablespoon rum or brandy
1 tablespoon soft brown sugar

1 Cut pineapple into eight bite-sized pieces. Cut peach into 8 wedges and slice banana. Thread all fruit on skewers; place in shallow dish.

2 To make Honey Cardamom Syrup, combine honey, butter, car- damom, rum and sugar in bowl. Pour mixture over kebabs, brush to coat. Cover; stand at room temperature 1 hour. Prepare and heat barbecue.

3 Cook the kebabs on a hot lightly greased barbecue flatplate for about 5 minutes. Brush with syrup while cooking. Serve drizzled with the remaining syrup. Top with a dollop of fresh cream or yoghurt, if desired.

1

2

3

TIPSY STRAWBERRY TRIFLE

Preparation time: 20 minutes
+ 4 hours refrigeration
Total cooking time: Nil
Serves 8

2 x 85 g (3 oz) packets red jelly crystals
1 cup (250 ml/8 fl oz) brandy or rum
1 cup (250 ml/8 fl oz) milk
2 x 250 g (8 oz) packets thin sponge finger biscuits

2 x 250 g (8 oz) punnets strawberries, hulled and sliced
3 cups (750 ml/24 fl oz) ready-made custard
1¼ cups (315 ml/10 fl oz) cream, whipped

1 Mix the jelly crystals with 1¾ cups (440 ml/14 fl oz) of boiling water and stir to dissolve. Pour into a shallow tin and refrigerate until the jelly has just set but is not firm.
2 Combine the brandy and milk in a dish. Dip half the biscuits in the brandy mixture then place in a single layer in a 3-litre glass or ceramic dish.

Spoon half the jelly over the biscuits. Scatter with half the strawberries and then half of the custard.
3 Dip the remaining sponge fingers in the brandy mixture and place evenly over the custard, followed by the remaining jelly and custard. Spread the whipped cream evenly over the custard and top with the remaining strawberries. Cover and refrigerate for 4 hours before serving.

Using a small sharp knife, hull the strawberries and cut into slices.

Spoon half the jelly over the biscuits before scattering on half the strawberries.

Dip the remaining biscuits in the brandy mixture and layer evenly over the custard.

BAKED CHEESECAKE

Preparation time: 30 minutes
+ 20 minutes refrigeration
+ chilling
Total cooking time: 55 minutes
Serves 8

250 g (8 oz) butternut cookies
1 teaspoon mixed spice
100 g (3½ oz) butter, melted
500 g (1 lb) cream cheese, softened
⅔ cup (160 g/5½ oz) caster sugar
4 eggs
1 teaspoon vanilla essence
1 tablespoon orange juice
1 tablespoon grated orange rind

TOPPING
1 cup (250 g/8 oz) sour cream
½ teaspoon vanilla essence
3 teaspoons orange juice
1 tablespoon caster sugar
freshly grated nutmeg

1 Lightly grease the base of a 20 cm (8 inch) springform tin. Finely crush the biscuits in a food processor for 30 seconds, or put them in a plastic bag and roll with a rolling pin. Transfer to a bowl and add the mixed spice and butter. Stir until all the crumbs are moistened, then spoon the mixture into the prepared tin and press it firmly into the base and sides. Refrigerate the case mixture for 20 minutes, or until firm.

2 Preheat the oven to moderate 180°C (350°F/Gas 4). Beat the cream cheese until smooth. Add the sugar and beat until smooth. Add the eggs, one at a time, beating well after each addition. Mix in the vanilla, orange juice and orange rind.
3 Pour the mixture into the crumb case and bake for 45 minutes, or until just firm. To make the topping, combine the sour cream, vanilla, orange juice and sugar in a mixing bowl. Spread this mixture over the hot cheesecake, sprinkle with nutmeg and return to the oven for 7 minutes. Cool, then refrigerate until firm.

Press the biscuit mixture into a springform tin with the back of a spoon.

Add the eggs one at a time to the cream cheese mixture and beat well.

When the filling is smooth, mix in the vanilla, orange juice and rind.

TIRAMISU

Preparation time: 30 minutes
+ 2 hours refrigeration
Total cooking time: Nil
Serves 6

3 cups (750 ml/24 fl oz) strong
black coffee, cooled
3 tablespoons Marsala or
    coffee-flavoured liqueur
2 eggs, separated
3 tablespoons caster sugar
250 g (8 oz) mascarpone
1 cup (250 ml/8 fl oz) cream, whipped

16 large sponge fingers
2 tablespoons dark cocoa powder

1 Mix together the coffee and
Marsala in a bowl and set aside.
Using electric beaters, beat the
egg yolks and sugar in a bowl for
3 minutes, or until thick and pale.
Add the mascarpone and mix until
just combined. Transfer to a large
bowl and fold in the cream.
2 Beat the egg whites until soft peaks
form. Fold quickly and lightly into
the cream mixture.
3 Dip half the biscuits into the coffee
mixture, then drain off any excess
coffee and arrange in the base of a

2.5 litre ceramic dish. Spread half the
cream mixture over the biscuits.
4 Dip the remaining biscuits into the
remaining coffee mixture and repeat
the layers. Smooth the surface and
dust liberally with the cocoa powder.
Refrigerate for at least 2 hours, or
until firm.

COOK'S FILE

Storage time: Tiramisu is best made
a day ahead to let the flavours develop.
Refrigerate until ready to serve.
Serving suggestion: Tiramisu is
delicious served with fresh fruit.

*Add the mascarpone to the egg yolks and
sugar and mix well.*

*Fold the beaten egg whites gently into
the cream mixture.*

*Dip half the biscuits in the coffee mixture,
drain, and arrange in the serving dish.*

ALMOND SEMI FREDDO

Preparation time: 30 minutes
+ 4 hours freezing
Total cooking time: Nil
Serves 8–10

300 ml cream
4 eggs, at room temperature,
    separated
²/₃ cup (85 g) icing sugar
¼ cup (60 ml) amaretto
½ cup (80 g) blanched almonds,
    toasted and chopped
8 amaretti biscuits, crushed

1 Whip the cream until firm peaks form, cover and refrigerate. Line a 10 x 21 cm loaf tin with plastic wrap so that it overhangs the 2 long sides.
2 Place the egg yolks and icing sugar in a large bowl and beat until pale and creamy. Whisk the egg whites in a separate bowl until firm peaks form. Stir the amaretto, almonds and amaretti biscuits into the egg yolk mixture, then carefully fold in the chilled cream and the egg whites until well combined. Carefully pour or spoon into the lined loaf tin and cover with the overhanging plastic. Freeze for 4 hours, or until frozen but not rock hard. Serve in slices with fresh fruit or a sprinkling of amaretto. The semifreddo can also be poured into individual moulds or serving dishes before freezing.

COOK'S FILE
Note: Semi freddo means semi-frozen, so if you want to leave it in the freezer overnight, remove it and place it in the refrigerator for 30 minutes to soften slightly before serving.
Hint: Serve the semi freddo with some fresh fruit or extra amaretto.

Place the amaretti biscuits in a plastic bag and crush with a rolling pin.

Beat the egg yolks and sugar together with electric beaters.

Carefully spoon the mixture into the lined loaf tin.

STRAWBERRIES WITH BALSAMIC VINEGAR

Preparation time: 10 minutes
+ 2 hours 30 minutes marinating
Total cooking time: Nil
Serves 4

750 g ripe small strawberries
¼ cup (60 g) caster sugar
2 tablespoons balsamic vinegar
½ cup (125 g) mascarpone

1 Wipe the strawberries with a clean damp cloth and carefully remove the green stalks. If the strawberries are large, cut each one in half.
2 Place all the strawberries in a large glass bowl, sprinkle the caster sugar evenly over the top and toss gently to coat. Set aside for 2 hours to macerate, then sprinkle the balsamic vinegar over the strawberries. Toss them again, then refrigerate for about 30 minutes.
3 Spoon the strawberries into four glasses, drizzle with the syrup and top with a dollop of mascarpone.

COOK'S FILE
Note: If you leave the strawberries for more than 2 hours, it is best to refrigerate them.
Hint: Thick cream or créme fraîche can be used instead of mascarpone.

Hull the strawberries after wiping clean with a damp cloth.

Sprinkle the caster sugar evenly over the strawberries.

Use good-quality balsamic vinegar to sprinkle over the strawberries.

CASSATA

Preparation time: 25 minutes +
overnight refrigeration
Total cooking time: 2 minutes
Serves 6

60 g blanched almonds, halved
30 g shelled pistachios
650 g fresh ricotta cheese (see Note)
½ cup (60 g) icing sugar
1½ teaspoons vanilla essence
2 teaspoons finely grated lemon rind
50 g cedro, chopped into 5 mm
   pieces (see Note)
50 g glacé orange, chopped into
   5 mm pieces
60 g red glacé cherries, halved
375 g ready-made round sponge
   cake, unfilled
½ cup (125 ml) Madeira or malmsey
   wine
14 blanched almonds, extra
14 red glacé cherries, extra, halved
icing sugar, for dusting
sweetened whipped cream, to serve

1 Dry-fry the almonds and
pistachios in a frying pan, tossing,
over medium heat for 2 minutes, or
until starting to change colour. Cool.
2 Press the ricotta cheese through a
sieve over a bowl. Stir in the icing
sugar, vanilla, lemon rind, cedro,
glacé orange, glacé cherries, almonds
and pistachios. Mix together well.
3 Grease a 1.25 litre pudding basin.
Cut the cake into 1 cm thick slices
horizontally. Set aside 1 round and
cut the rest into wedges, trimming
the base to make triangles. Sprinkle
the cut side of the triangles lightly
with Madeira and arrange around the
base and side of the bowl, cut-side-
down, trimming if necessary to fit.
Spoon the ricotta mixture into the
centre. Top with a layer of sponge
cake. Press down firmly and neaten
the rough edges, if necessary.
Refrigerate overnight.
4 Carefully unmould onto a serving
plate. Arrange the extra almonds and
cherries on top and dust with icing
sugar just before serving. Serve with
sweetened whipped cream, which can
be piped in patterns over the cassata
for a true Sicilian look.

COOK'S FILE

Note: It is important to use fresh ricotta
from the deli so it can be moulded
successfully. Cedro is candied citron
peel and is available from most Italian
delicatessens. If unavailable, use glacé
pineapple and ½ teaspoon finely grated
lemon rind.

*Arrange the pieces of sponge cake around
the base and side of the bowl.*

*Spoon the ricotta mixture into the cake-
lined pudding basin.*

*Top with a layer of sponge cake, press
down firmly and neaten any edges.*

COCONUT LIME ICE CREAM

Preparation time: 10 minutes
+ 30 minutes freezing
Total cooking time: Nil
Serves 4

½ cup (25 g) desiccated coconut
1½ tablespoons grated lime rind
⅓ cup (80 ml) lime juice
4 tablespoons coconut milk powder
1 litre good-quality vanilla ice cream,
   softened
coconut macaroon biscuits,
   to serve

1 Place the desiccated coconut, grated lime rind, lime juice and coconut milk powder in a bowl, and mix together well.
2 Add the coconut mixture to the ice cream and fold through with a large metal spoon until evenly incorporated. Work quickly so that the ice cream does not melt. Return the mixture to the freezer and freeze for 30 minutes to firm. To serve, place 3 scoops in four latté glasses and serve with some coconut macaroons on the side.

APPLE AND PEAR SORBET

Preparation time: 10 minutes
+ freezing
Total cooking time: 10 minutes
Serves 4–6

4 large green apples, peeled, cored
and chopped
4 pears, peeled, cored and chopped
1 piece of lemon rind (1.5 cm x 4 cm)
1 cinnamon stick
¼ cup (60 ml) lemon juice
4 tablespoons caster sugar
2 tablespoons Calvados or poire
    William liqueur (optional)

1 Place the apple and pear in a large
deep saucepan with the lemon rind,
cinnamon stick and enough water to
just cover the fruit. Cover and poach
the fruit gently over medium–low heat
for 6–8 minutes, or until tender.
Remove the lemon rind and
cinnamon stick. Place the fruit in a
food processor and blend with the
lemon juice until smooth.
2 Place the sugar in a saucepan with
⅓ cup (80 ml) water, bring to the boil
and simmer for 1 minute. Add the
fruit purée and the liqueur and
combine well.
3 Pour into a shallow metal tray and
freeze for 2 hours, or until the mixture
is frozen around the edges. Transfer to
a food processor or bowl and blend or
beat until smooth. Pour back into the
tray and return to the freezer. Repeat
this process three times. For the final
freezing, place in an airtight container
—cover the surface with a piece of
greaseproof paper and cover with a
lid. Serve in small glasses or bowls.

COOK'S FILE

Notes: The length of cooking time to
poach the apple and pear will depend
on the ripeness of the fruit.
Pour an extra nip of Calvados over the
sorbet to serve, if desired.

*Check if the fruit is tender by using the
tip of a sharp knife.*

*Blend the partially frozen mixture in a
food processor until smooth.*

SUMMER FRUIT COMPOTE

Preparation time: 15 minutes
+ 3 hours refrigeration
Total cooking time: 5 minutes
Serves 6

2 cups (500 g) caster sugar
3 cups (750 ml) white wine, such as
    Chardonnay
2 teaspoons finely grated
    lime rind
¼ cup (60 ml) lime juice
2 mangoes
3 freestone peaches
3 nectarines
vanilla ice cream, to serve

1 Place the sugar, white wine, lime rind and juice in a large saucepan. Stir over low heat for 3 minutes, or until the sugar has dissolved. Bring to the boil, then reduce the heat and simmer for 2 minutes. Keep warm.
2 Cut the cheeks from the mangoes, then remove the skin. Cut each mango cheek into 6 thick wedges. Place the mango in a large serving bowl. Cut a cross in one end of the peaches and nectarines, and plunge them into a bowl of boiling water, and then into cold water. Peel and cut into 4 wedges each, discarding the stones. Add to the mango.
3 Pour the warm syrup over the fruit, and refrigerate, covered, for 2–3 hours. To serve, return to room temperature and serve with ice cream.

COOK'S FILE

Note: You can leave the peaches and nectarines unpeeled, if preferred.

1

2

3

CHERRY CLAFOUTIS

Preparation time: 15 minutes
Total cooking time: 40 minutes
Serves 6–8

500 g fresh cherries
(see Hint)
³/₄ cup (90 g) plain flour
2 eggs, lightly beaten
¹/₃ cup (90 g) caster sugar
1 cup (250 ml) milk
¹/₄ cup (60 ml) thick cream
50 g unsalted butter, melted
icing sugar, for dusting

1 Preheat the oven to moderate 180°C (350°F/Gas 4). Lightly brush a 1.5 litre ovenproof dish with melted butter.
2 Carefully pit the cherries, then spread into the dish in a single layer.
3 Sift the flour into a bowl, add the eggs and whisk until smooth. Add the sugar, milk, cream and butter, whisking until just combined, but being careful not to overbeat.
4 Pour the batter over the cherries and bake for 30–40 minutes, or until a skewer comes out clean when inserted into the centre. Remove from the oven and dust generously with icing sugar. Serve immediately

COOK'S FILE

Hint: You can use a 720 g jar of cherries. Make sure you thoroughly drain the juice away.
Variation: Blueberries, blackberries, raspberries, or small, well-flavoured strawberries can be used. A delicious version can be made using slices of poached pear.

Add the sugar, milk, cream and butter to the flour mixture and whisk well.

Pour the batter over the single layer of cherries.

Cook until the batter is golden brown and nicely set.

COFFEE CREAM PAVLOVA ROLL

Preparation time: 30 minutes
+ cooling time
Total cooking time: 30 minutes
Serves 6–8

MERINGUE

4 egg whites, at room temperature
¾ cup (185 g) caster sugar
1 teaspoon vanilla essence
2 teaspoons white vinegar
2 teaspoons cornflour
⅓ cup (30 g) flaked almonds
1 tablespoon caster sugar, to
    sprinkle, extra

TOFFEE PRALINE

⅓ cup (30 g) flaked almonds
1⅓ cups (340 g) caster sugar

COFFEE CREAM

½ cup (125 ml) cream
4–5 tablespoons very strong cold
    black coffee
2 tablespoons icing sugar
250 g mascarpone

1 Preheat the oven to warm 160°C (315°F/Gas 2–3). Lightly grease a 30 x 25 cm swiss roll tin and line the base and sides with baking paper. To make the Meringue, beat the egg whites in a dry bowl until firm peaks form. Gradually beat in the sugar, beating for 5–8 minutes, or until the sugar has dissolved and the mixture is thick and glossy. Fold in the vanilla, vinegar and cornflour, then spread into the prepared tin and smooth the top. Sprinkle with almonds, then bake for 20 minutes, or until firm.

2 Meanwhile, to make the Toffee Praline, cover a baking tray with baking paper and sprinkle with almonds. Put the sugar and ½ cup (125 ml) water in a small saucepan and stir over low heat until the sugar dissolves. Bring to the boil and simmer without stirring until the toffee is dark golden—watch carefully as it can burn quickly. Pour over the almonds and leave until set. Break into small pieces or pulverise in a food processor. Set aside.

3 Put a large sheet of baking paper on a work surface and sprinkle with the extra caster sugar. Invert the meringue onto the paper so that the almonds are on the bottom. Peel off the lining paper and leave for 10 minutes.

4 To make the Coffee Cream, beat the cream in a small bowl until firm peaks form. Gently stir in the coffee, icing sugar and mascarpone and mix. Do not overbeat or it will curdle. Spread the meringue with the coffee cream and roll up firmly. Transfer to a plate. Sprinkle the toffee praline down the centre of the log, slice and serve.

Evenly spread the meringue into the swiss roll tin and smooth the top.

Pour the toffee over the almonds on the baking tray.

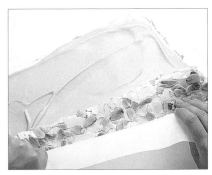

Roll up the pavlova firmly, using the baking paper to help you.

QUICK DESSERTS

When you are busy with a barbecue, dessert is often a low priority. These delicious hot and cold sweets, however, take little time to prepare and are the perfect finish for any party.

CHOCOLATE CHERRY PARFAIT

Chocolate ice cream (1–2 scoops each)
Choc-chip ice cream (1–2 scoops each)
400 g can pitted black cherries, drained
⅓ cup (80 ml) good-quality chocolate sauce
Dark chocolate cherry bar, chopped, to garnish

Divide the two ice creams and cherries among four parfait glasses. Drizzle with the chocolate sauce and garnish with the chocolate cherry bar. Serve at once. Serves 4.

BANANA CARAMEL ICE CREAM STACK

400 g pound cake, cut into 8 slices about 1.5 cm thick
4 rectangular slabs vanilla ice cream
2 large bananas, cut on the diagonal into 1 cm slices
3 tablespoons good-quality caramel sauce,
        plus extra to drizzle
⅓ cup (50 g) honey-roasted macadamia nuts,
        chopped, plus extra, to garnish

Place a slice of cake on each of four serving plates, then top each slice with an ice cream slab. Divide the banana slices, caramel sauce and chopped nuts among each serving, then top with another slice of cake. Drizzle with extra caramel sauce and scatter with the extra nuts. Serve immediately. Serves 4.

Note: Any unused cake can be frozen.

LITTLE MANGO PASSIONFRUIT TRIFLES

60 g plain sponge cake, cut into 1 cm pieces
2 tablespoons Cointreau
2 small or 1 large mango, cut into bite-sized slices
2 tablespoons passionfruit pulp
1/2 cup (125 ml) ready-made vanilla custard
200 g mascarpone
1 tablespoon icing sugar
Passionfruit pulp, extra, to garnish (optional)

Divide the cake pieces among four tall glasses (about
1¼ cups/310 ml). Drizzle 2 teaspoons Cointreau over
the cake in each glass, then leave for 5 minutes. Arrange
half the mango on the cake. Divide the passionfruit pulp
and custard evenly among the glasses, then top with the
remaining mango slices. Gently combine the mascarpone
and icing sugar until light and creamy. Just before serving,
dollop the marscapone mixture on top and garnish with
extra passionfruit. Serve at once. Serves 4.

Note: Another 1–2 tablespoons of custard can replace the
layer of mascarpone, if preferred.

MELON WITH LEMON GRASS SYRUP

1/4 cup (60 g) caster sugar
3 fresh kaffir lime leaves
2 lemon grass stems (white part only), bruised
2 thin slices fresh ginger
250 g watermelon, seeded and peeled
250 g honeydew melon
250 g rockmelon
12 lychees, peeled

Heat the sugar and 1 cup (250 ml) water in a small
saucepan over medium heat and stir until the sugar has
dissolved. Add the lime leaves, lemon grass and ginger,
and simmer rapidly for 5–7 minutes, or until thickened.
Cool completely. Cut each melon into 2 cm cubes, then
place in a large bowl with the lychees. Discard the lime
leaves, lemon grass and ginger from the syrup. Pour the
syrup over the fruit and serve with vanilla ice cream, if
desired. Serves 4.

Hint: The longer the fruit sits in the syrup, the better—the
flavours will develop as the fruit becomes infused with the
syrup. It will store well for up to 3 days in the refrigerator.

SUMMER DRINKS

PINEAPPLE CRUSH

Peel and cube a pineapple and place it in a blender with 2 cups (270 g) crushed ice. Blend until smooth and then add to a bowl with 1 litre ginger beer and stir to mix. Serve with a fresh piece of pineapple for garnish. Serves 4

FROZEN PASSIONFRUIT MARGARITA

Put 80 ml tequila, 30 ml Cointreau, 40 ml lime juice and the sieved pulp and juice of 6 passionfruit in a blender with 1 cup (135 g) crushed ice and whizz together. Dip the rim of 2 glasses in lemon juice and salt, then pour in the margarita. Garnish with lime slices. Serves 2

PEACH CUP

Cut 2 ripe peaches in half, remove the stones and slice thinly. Put in a bowl with 1 bottle (750 ml) peach brandy, 750 ml peach juice, 1 bottle sparkling rosé and 1 bottle soda water. Stir together and serve garnished with mint sprigs. Serves 12

STRAWBERRY CHAMPAGNE PUNCH

Hull and slice 250 g strawberries and place them in a punch bowl. Add 50 g caster sugar, ½ cup (125 ml) Grand Marnier or Cointreau and 30 ml Grenadine and leave to stand. Just before serving, add 2 bottles chilled Champagne and 1 bottle soda water. Serves 12

WATERMELON COOLER

Cut ½ large or 1 small watermelon into pieces and remove the seeds. Put in a blender with 1–2 cm fresh ginger and 1 cup (250 ml) orange juice and blend until smooth. Pour over crushed ice to serve. (For a decorative effect, cut a slice off the top of the watermelon and scoop out the inside, and use this as a serving bowl for the finished drink.) Serve in highball glasses. Serves 4

MINT JULEP

Place the rind of 3 lemons in a pan with 1 cup (250 g) sugar and 1 cup (250 ml) water. Dissolve the sugar slowly and bring to the boil. Reduce the heat and simmer for 5 minutes, then strain and leave to cool. Juice the lemons, as well as another 2 lemons. Place 4 cups (540 g) crushed ice and 1 cup (20 g) mint leaves in a food processor and whizz briefly to crush the mint. Tip into a large chilled bowl and add the lemon syrup, lemon juice and ½ cup (125 ml) whisky. Dip the rims of martini glasses in lemon juice and sugar, pour in the julep and garnish with mint sprigs.
Serves 8–10

PEACH FIZZ

Cut a cross in the base of 6 freestone peaches. Plunge into a large bowl of boiling water. Carefully remove with a slotted spoon and place in a bowl of cold water. Peel away the skin, remove the stone and chop the flesh. Place in a blender or food processor with 2 cups (500 ml) chilled white wine and ¼ cup (60 g) caster sugar. Blend until smooth. Place ice cubes in 6 tall glasses and pour in the peach mixture. Top with a mint leaf.
Serves 6

KIWI PINE SPARKLER

Peel 4 kiwi fruit, place in a blender or food processor and blend until smooth. Add 2 cups (500 ml) tropical fruit juice and 1 cup (250 ml) pineapple juice and blend until combined. Chill. Pour over ice cubes into 6 large tumblers. Top with chilled sparkling mineral water. Add chopped strawberries, kiwi fruit and small mint leaves. Add a dash of Pimms for something alcoholic.
Serves 6

CHAMPAGNE COCKTAIL

Place a sugar cube and ½ teaspoon grenadine in each of 6 Champagne glasses. Top with Champagne and place half a fresh strawberry in each glass. Serve immediately.
Serves 6

Left, from top: Peach fizz, Kiwi pine sparkler, Champagne cocktail. Right, from top: Grape refresher; Mango summer haze, Vodka and lime frappé.

GRAPE REFRESHER

Place ¼ cup (60 ml) caster sugar and 1 litre dark grape juice in a large saucepan and stir over medium heat until the sugar has dissolved. Stir through ¼ cup (60 ml) lemon juice and refrigerate until cold. Place some ice cubes in 6 tall glasses, pour over the grape mix to three quarters full and top with sparkling mineral water and a lemon slice. Cut 12 seedless green grapes in half, thread among 6 wooden skewers and arrange over each glass.
Serves 6

MANGO SUMMER HAZE

Peel 2 mangoes and cut the flesh away from the stone. Place in a blender with 2 cups (500 ml) orange juice and ¼ cup (60 g) caster sugar. Blend until smooth. Add 2 cups (500 ml) chilled sparkling mineral water. Pour into 6 tall glasses and top with ice cubes, if desired. Add a dash of white rum for something a little more daring. Garnish with fresh mango slices, if desired.
Serves 6

VODKA AND LIME FRAPPÉ

Blend 40 ice cubes in a blender until just crushed. Divide among 6 small glasses and pour 30 ml vodka and 20 ml lime juice cordial into each of the glasses. Stir lightly and serve immediately.
Serves 6

INDEX

A

USEFUL INFORMATION

All our recipes are thoroughly tested. Standard metric measuring cups and spoons are used in the development of our recipes. All cup and spoon measurements are level. We have used 60 g eggs in all recipes. Sizes of cans vary from manufacturer to manufacturer and between countries—use the can size closest to the one suggested in the recipe.

CONVERSION GUIDE

1 cup	= 250 ml (8 fl oz)
1 teaspoon	= 5 ml
1 Australian tablespoon	= 20 ml (4 teaspoons)
1 UK/US tablespoon	= 15 ml (3 teaspoons)

Dry Measures	Liquid Measures	Linear Measures
30 g = 1 oz	30 ml = 1 fl oz	6 mm = ¼ inch
250 g = 8 oz	125 ml = 4 fl oz	1 cm = ½ inch
500 g = 1 lb	250 ml = 8 fl oz	2.5 cm = 1 inch

CUP CONVERSIONS—DRY INGREDIENTS

1 cup almonds, slivered	= 125 g (4 oz)
whole	= 155 g (5 oz)
1 cup cheese, lightly packed	= 125 g (4 oz)
processed cheddar	= 155 g (5 oz)
1 cup flour, plain, or self-raising	= 125 g (4 oz)
wholemeal	= 140 g (4½ oz)
1 cup minced beef or pork	= 250 g (8 oz)
1 cup pasta shapes	= 125 g (4 oz)
1 cup raisins	= 170 g (5½ oz)
1 cup rice, short grain, raw	= 200 g (6½ oz)
1 cup sesame seeds	= 160 g (5 oz)
1 cup split peas	= 250 g (8 oz)

OVEN TEMPERATURES

Where temperature ranges are indicated, the lower figure applies to gas ovens, the higher to electric ovens. This allows for the fact that the flame in gas ovens generates a drier heat, which effectively cooks food faster than the moister heat of an electric oven, even if the temperature setting is the same.

	°C	°F	Gas Mark
Very slow	120	250	½
Slow	150	300	2
Mod slow	160	325	3
Moderate	180	350	4
Mod hot	190(g) – 210(e)	375 – 425	5
Hot	200(g) – 240(e)	400 – 475	6
Very hot	230(g) – 260(e)	450 – 525	8

(g) = gas (e) = electric

Note: For fan-forced ovens, check your appliance manual, but as a general rule, set the oven temperature to 20°C lower than the temperature indicated in the recipe.

INTERNATIONAL GLOSSARY

capsicum	sweet bell pepper
chick pea	garbanzo bean
cornflour	cornstarch
eggplant	aubergine
plain flour	all-purpose flour
spring onion	scallion
zucchini	courgette

First published in 2003 by Murdoch Books Pty Limited,
Erico House, 6th Floor North, 93-99 Upper Richmond Road, Putney, London SW15 2TG.

This edition published in 2007 for Index Books Ltd,
Garrard Way, Kettering, Northants, NN16 8TD

ISBN 978 1 74196 016 7

Managing Editor: Anna Cheifetz **Design Manager:** Helen Taylor **Food Editors:** Kerrie Ray, Tracy Rutherford
Photographers: Jon Bader, Reg Morrison (steps) **Food Stylist:** Carolyn Fienberg **Food Preparation:** Jo Forrest
Chief Executive: Juliet Rogers **Production Manager:** Lucy Byrne
Colour separation by Colourscan, Singapore. **Printed and bound** in Singapore by Imago